The Ethics of Business in a Global Economy

Issues in Business Ethics

VOLUME 4

The Ethics of Business in a Global Economy

edited by

PAUL M. MINUS
The Council for Ethics in Economics
Columbus, Ohio, USA

with contributions from

M. Cherif Bassiouni
Richard G. Capen, Jr.
Joanne B. Ciulla
Richard T. De George
Thomas Donaldson
Wilfried Guth
Shunji Hosaka
Jack Mahoney
Karen Marquiss
Yukimasa Nagayasu
Stephen O'Brien
Amartya Sen
Meir Tamari
Hiroyuki Yoshino

Kluwer Academic Publishers
Boston / Dordrecht / London

Distributors for North America:
Kluwer Academic Publishers
101 Philip Drive
Assinippi Park
Norwell, Massachusetts 02061 USA

Distributors for all other countries:
Kluwer Academic Publishers Group
Distribution Centre
Post Office Box 322
3300 AH Dordrecht, THE NETHERLANDS

Library of Congress Cataloging-in-Publication Data

The Ethics of business in a global economy / edited by Paul M. Minus ;
   with contributions from M. Cherif Bassiouni ... [et al.].
       p.   cm. -- (Issues in business ethics ; v. 4)
     Includes bibliographical references and index.
     ISBN 0-7923-9334-1
     1. Business ethics--Cross-cultural studies. 2. Business-
-Religious aspects. I. Minus, Paul M. II. Bassiouni, M. Cherif,
1937-   . III. Series.
HF5387.E858 1993
174'.4--dc20   93-7110
                                                     CIP

Printed on acid-free paper.

Printed in the United States of America

CONTENTS

1

Introduction

Paul M. Minus

Overview

The papers gathered in this volume were first presented for
reflection and discussion at a landmark event in March 1992. The
International Conference on the Ethics of Business in a Global
Economy, held in Columbus, Ohio, brought together over 300
participants from twenty-two nations in six continents. This was the
most geographically diverse body of leaders ever assembled to
consider issues of ethics in business. Approximately two-thirds of
them were business executives; the others came mainly from the fields
of education and religion.

Knowing the context from which this book emerged will help
readers understand its composition and content. As can be quickly
seen, the fourteen authors who have contributed to it come from
different areas of the world and from different fields of endeavor.
One finds, first, essays on the book's central theme by business
leaders from four nations. Next there are analyses of three key topics
by scholars active in the fields of economics and ethics. Then come
statements by practitioners of four major world religions on the
relevance of their respective traditions to the ethics of business.
Finally there are six brief case studies prepared by two business
ethicists about specific ethical issues arising in international business.

The authors address different facets of one of the most
dramatic new facts of our time: the globalization of business. With
many corporations now operating around the world and others
planning a significant expansion of markets, this development is
destined to accelerate in coming decades.

P.M. Minus (ed.), *The Ethics of Business in a Global Economy.*

International operations create fresh opportunities and problems for business executives. Attention must be paid to difficult questions that arise when corporations cross national and cultural boundaries, establishing far-reaching patterns of interdependence. Prominent among those questions are the ones focusing upon development of internationally shared values and standards that are necessary both for economic success and public acceptance. How far can business leaders go toward establishing an international consensus regarding ethical standards for business conduct? How can these standards be effectively implemented by their respective companies? How can the standards constructively influence the quality of global economic competition?

The deliberate diversity of geography and perspective among contributors to this volume points to its essential (albeit implicit) thesis: that as business firms around the world increasingly operate in a global economy, moving beyond their accustomed places and practices, it is critically important that insights from different cultures and different disciplines be brought to bear on the development of ethical vision and ethical conduct that fit this new situation.

New interest in ethical business practice

A rich resource for addressing this need has been created by the rise of interest in ethical business practice that has occurred in recent years among people in the fields of business, education and religion. The causes of this fresh interest are multiple and complex, and the precise pattern of contributing factors varies from nation to nation. Among the major factors accounting for it are frequent media revelations of business misconduct; rising public pressure for socially responsible business practices; changing patterns of governmental regulation; and growing recognition of the relevance of ethics for successful business enterprise.

Evident first in the United States in the 1970s, the upsurge of interest in ethical business now has spread into Europe and other parts of the world. It can be seen widely among business executives—for example, in the formulation of ethics codes by corporations; in ethics reports by such influential business organizations as The Conference Board in the United States, Confindustria in Italy, and Keidanren in Japan; and in the growing activity of such bodies as ACADI in France (Association des Cadres Dirigeants de l'Industrie pour le progrès social et économique), the Institute of Business Ethics in England, and the Ethics Resource Center in the United States.

A parallel development also is evident among scholars involved in the rapid rise of the new discipline of business ethics. Many business schools now offer courses in the field and some have established endowed chairs of business ethics. Scholarly journals and professional societies (such as the Society for Business Ethics and the European Business Ethics Network) are devoted to this subject, and a substantial body of literature is emerging. Indeed, the series in which this volume appears is a sign of the latter development.

Leaders in religion have manifested a similar interest. Significant initiatives among Christians in Western Europe and North America, for example, have taken a variety of forms. Some of them have tended toward a confrontational approach to business, as seen in the activity of the Interfaith Center for Corporate Responsibility in the United States. Other groups have sought to bring Christian business leaders together to explore the implications of their faith for business, as in the Christian Association of Business Executives in Britain, and the two dozen widely scattered national affiliates of Uniapac (International Christian Union of Business Executives), based in Brussels. Theologians and religious ethicists have also turned their attention to questions of ethical business and economics; the work of Roman Catholic educational institutions, such as the University of Notre Dame, has been especially striking.

A time for dialogue

As yet, the work of these three groups usually has flowed in separate channels, with little active dialogue or collaboration among them. This book (and the conference that generated it) are testimony to the belief that the time has come to bridge the different "worlds" inhabited by people in these three fields, and that the effort to do so is extremely important. Each of the groups can offer insights crucial to understanding the managerial, historical, sociological, economic, psychological and philosophical complexities of the problem of ethical business and to formulating effective steps forward.

But this partnership is not easy to achieve. In our modern compartmentalized society, each of the three groups is accustomed to its particular way of doing things and of thinking and talking about what it does. Each has its own culture and its own sense of self-importance. Hence, moving beyond the separation requires careful, persistent effort, in which all participants learn to "listen" attentively to each other and to "translate" their jargon into language accessible to outsiders.

Although such dialogue is not easily achieved, experience demonstrates that it can happen. Here and there successful efforts have been made in recent years to build the requisite bridges, and some traffic has begun to flow across them. Mention can be made only briefly of the Council for Ethics in Economics (CEE), based in Columbus, Ohio, whose ten-year experience of interdisciplinary exchange underlies the planning that occurred for the March 1992 conference and for this book. Those of us engaged in this association of leaders in business, education and religion have been given a taste of the fruits that can emerge from the dialogical process. People on all sides have come to a fresh appreciation of what each partner brings to the table: the executive's experience of the rich texture and complex processes of business organizations; the scholar's knowledge of the wider realities that affect business; and the religionist's appreciation of the dramas being played out in every business person's heart and on the stage of history. We have seen that much can be done by working collaboratively to strengthen the ethical fabric of business and economic life.

The papers in this volume represent not the end product of an interdisciplinary, international dialogue but significant first steps toward its beginning. Readers thus have essentially the same opportunity as did conference participants in March 1992: to learn what distinguished leaders from different regions and different fields think about varied facets of an important topic, to look for points of agreement and disagreement, then to use these learnings as building blocks for shaping one's own enhanced understanding of the ethical business practice appropriate in a global economy. The six cases in the final section of the volume give readers the further challenge of testing and refining their understandings by asking what decisions they would make in response to the tough business situations presented there; and when used in group settings, the cases can become fertile ground for an inductive process of sharpening issues and building consensus.

Some gleanings

Individual readers inevitably will be struck by different points in each chapter and will bring away different conclusions from the volume as a whole. By way of stimulating that process, it may be useful for me to summarize a few key messages I have gleaned from each author, as well as points of contact I have noted among authors and questions they have prompted for my further reflection.

Stephen O'Brien's stage-setting essay recognizes that with the fall of communism, a historic turn has been taken by the world and a promising opportunity opened up for business. Reflecting his successful experience in the British organization called Business in the Community, he is strikingly optimistic about the prospect of corporations, through pursuit of their own self-interest, becoming a powerful agent for social justice: they can build new markets for their products and services by helping to build up disadvantaged people and societies. There is a potentially useful role for religion, he believes, in helping business properly approach this reconstructive task.

The pieces by Wilfried Guth, Hiroyuki Yoshino and Richard Capen show intriguing points both of convergence and divergence. One may wonder if the outlooks of executives of large companies in Germany, Japan and the United States are so similar that each of the three essays could have been written by thoughtful executives in any one of the three countries. On the other hand, it may well be true (as some commentators noted when first hearing these papers presented) that there is something characteristically German in Guth's attention to the wider social context of business enterprise, something characteristically Japanese in Yoshino's focus upon his own corporation, and something very American in Capen's strong emphasis upon individual values.

I am particularly struck by the priority the three executives assign to several ethical frontiers which most business ethicists have not yet addressed in major ways. Both Guth and Capen, for example, stress the importance for developing a *corporation's* ethics of the values and virtues of the *individuals* who lead the corporation. How should such persons understand their role of ethical leadership? What wisdom do the ethical traditions provide for helping them fulfill it? The religious traditions? I wonder, too, how more intellectual attention can be mustered for the several practical ethical tasks that Yoshino and Guth consider key—for what the former, for example, calls "business ethics at the shop-floor level"?

The contributions by Professors Sen, Donaldson and De George are skillfully crafted analyses of issues crucial to the serious pursuit of ethical practice by businesses anywhere in the world. Amartya Sen's contention that economics and ethics belong together is a significant step from the side of economics toward overcoming the regrettable modern separation between the two fields noted earlier in Guth's essay. The position charted by Thomas Donaldson between cultural relativism and ethical absolutism provides a promising path for thoughtful executives who face tough questions about how to reconcile the differences between "home" and "foreign" values encountered in their international operations. And Richard De George's overview of the diverse relations existing internationally between business and governments helps one appreciate the variability of that relationship, as well as the potentially positive role that can be played in shaping business conduct by those of us who constitute what De George calls the "neglected third party."

The four brief essays by Buddhist, Jewish, Christian and Muslim authors represent modest first steps in what many hope will become a long journey toward increased interreligious understanding and collaboration on the economic and business fronts. Clearly, much work needs to be done yet by each religious tradition to make its key ethical teachings accessible to outsiders. The essential prerequisite for that task perhaps is for each tradition to make those teachings accessible and pertinent to its practitioners who work in the business arena. Doing so may well be a decisive contribution toward providing the ingredients necessary for helping many executives around the world embody the kind of personal virtues and values alluded to earlier.

The cases prepared by Karen Marquiss and Joanne Ciulla represent a different approach to reflection about ethics in business. The case method is increasingly used to help students and experienced managers alike think about the kinds of ethical questions and dilemmas encountered in the business world. These six cases reflect a wide variety of circumstances, and they raise a fairly typical spectrum of ethical questions arising today in international business operations. Addressing them should help readers improve the quality of their ethical reasoning and decision-making.

I suggested earlier that these essays can be viewed as the first steps of an international, interdisciplinary dialogue. I believe they are substantial first steps, for they reveal minds and hearts creatively engaged in a great new enterprise. But as the process moves forward in the future, other voices need to be heard. For example, more needs to be learned from those whom Stephen O'Brien calls "the poor and oppressed" and those whom Richard De George calls "the neglected third party." Perhaps their additions to the dialogue will help provide a clearer sense of what can be gained by seeking to strengthen the ethical dimensions of business as it operates in the new global economy. What "rewards" will there be for individuals in business, for their organizations, for their communities, for the post-communist world, for future generations? And what may be the consequences of failure to move toward this goal?

It is encouraging to know that these questions—along with other key ones raised implicitly and explicitly by the contributors to this volume—are now being pursued by resourceful individuals and institutions around the world. For its part, the Council for Ethics in Economics takes very seriously its responsibility to continue the dialogue begun in March 1992, and a major international project to that end is currently unfolding under its direction.

I am grateful to the fourteen authors who contributed to this volume, and to all those whose variety of other contributions have helped bring it to fruition. With them I look forward to a future harvest.

Part I

Business Perspectives

2

The Ethical Challenge to Business in a New Era for Market Economies

Stephen O'Brien

Echoes from Davos

The issue I shall address to begin our inquiry has been much on the minds of world leaders in recent times. In fact, two of them spoke about this issue at the 1992 session of the World Economic Forum in Davos, Switzerland. Their words aptly set the stage for what I want to say.

Here, first, is an excerpt from the Davos speech of Czech leader Vacláv Havel:

> We all know that our civilization is in danger....The paradox at the moment is that man—the great collector of information—is well aware of all this, yet is absolutely incapable of dealing with the danger.... We are trying to deal with what we have unleashed by employing the same means we used to unleash it in the first place....Everything suggests that this is not the way to go. What is needed is something different, something greater. Man's attitude to the world must be radically changed....The point is that we should fundamentally change how we behave.

The other statement is from the Davos speech of the Prince of Wales, with whom I am privileged to work in his capacity as President of the London-based organization, Business in the Community.

P.M. Minus (ed.), *The Ethics of Business in a Global Economy*.

It is one thing, of course, to have brought the Cold War to an end; it is quite another to bring about the adjustments necessary to convert that success into a better life for all of the people concerned, and to remain on guard against other threats which, if we are not extraordinarily careful, could so easily undermine the achievements of the last few years....

We all have an interest in making a success of the transition and indeed in working further to improve the functioning of our own societies and economies....

All I want to emphasize is that, as it says in the Bible, "Man does not live by bread alone." We are not just cost-effective machines that can be made ever more efficient. There is another dimension that has to be recognized, and that is why the message I want to leave you with today is that business is uniquely placed to take a lead and to help create that vital balance in our lives—but doing so in partnership with local communities, with government, non-governmental organizations and other representatives of the voluntary sector.

As I now move further in the direction that Prince Charles has pointed us, I hope to fuse together several ideas that have seemed totally separated. These ideas are, firstly, the power of the international corporation; secondly, business ethics; and thirdly, perhaps more surprising, liberation theology. The task for me is to see if there is some way that, against the backdrop of communism's collapse, these can be mixed in such a way as to produce a vision for a new thrust toward social justice that is of great benefit both to business and to the wider society.

Changing perceptions of multinationals

Twenty years ago I attended a conference in Cambridge, England, convened by a body known as the "Industrial Christian Fellowship." It was to be a far-sighted attempt by those of us who saw ourselves as the inheritors of F. D. Maurice and the Christian Socialist Movement to impress the big battalions of business with our concern for their ethics and especially for the way that so many of them appeared to be riding roughshod over Third World development and the other causes dear to our hearts. As it turned out, we were convincingly vanquished, and to this day I can hear the superior tones of the conference chairman, a leading investment banker, declaring in his summary statement that "earnings per share is the name of the game and this is the only game." In other words, businesses' only role was to be concerned with profit.

But what on earth would my 1972 investment banker have made of the spontaneous and prolonged standing ovation recently given by the world's business leaders in Davos to Prince Charles following his challenge to them to work collaboratively with other sectors to improve social and economic conditions around the world?

If this speech and the reaction to it failed to cause my investment banker to turn in his grave, then surely that must have happened following the statement in 1991 by Prime Minister John Major (supposedly a conservative leader) that the involvement by business in its communities at all levels is "a revolution I unreservedly welcome."

Twenty years ago the emerging multinational company was something of a social pariah. It was, we were told, outside all forms of political control and a potential threat to national sovereignty. Its principal purpose was the rape of the domestic economy and the repatriation of profit. It was held to bolster morally bankrupt regimes and to ransom honest consumers by the use of cartels and monopolies. The multinational was essentially a threat from the outside, while our own British businesses, trading successfully overseas, heroically battled to make profit against impossible odds such as tariff barriers, foreign prejudices, and currency variations invented by foreigners. This caricature was fueled, in Britain at least, by the oil crisis of the early 1970s. Somehow the emerging multinationals were identified as being part of an Arab conspiracy to hike the price of a key energy resource and thus not only to endanger the economy but also to undermine our parliamentary democracy itself.

Twenty years later, the picture looks quite different and infinitely more hopeful. The multinational corporation is no longer an alien invader but a positive force, perhaps the only positive force, with a vested interest in raising living standards and therefore fostering social justice across the entire globe. It is an engine of change whose time has come.

A new situation

There are many familiar factors that have caused this shift, and they have nothing to do with simply behaving better, although better behavior increasingly brings its own harvest of reward. Topping any list of the factors bringing change must be the phenomenal speeding up of communications and the part they play in creating a global market for information and ideas. The legendary Chicago taxi driver can monitor his investments in the European and Far Eastern stock markets, arbitraging freely between them if he wants to on a real time basis, and around the clock if he wants to stay awake. Television has played a major role. We all had a grandstand view in August 1991 of the attempted coup in Moscow, and just a few months earlier we had watched the sickening progress of Scud missiles from our armchairs in much the same way as we British had followed the ball to the boundary as England succumbed to West Indian pressure on the cricket field. The decision to allow television into South Africa surely accelerated the process of change there, because it grew harder and harder to conceal the world's reaction to the apartheid regime.

Just as there has developed a global market for information and ideas, so there has emerged one global market for products and services. For example, Lord Laing, the chairman of United Biscuits (one of our great British companies), recently said that the economy of the developed world was approaching a saturation point for one of his products, digestive biscuits; hence if his company wanted to expand the sale of this product, it would have to see the developing world as the marketplace of the future.

As companies in recent years have begun to realize that there is a single world market, they simultaneously have become aware of a new pressure on them—the power of the consumer. The early success of boycotts in the southern United States to hasten the process of desegregation prompted the use of sanctions more widely, for it brought the realization that powerful forces for freedom existed that no business could possibly withstand and remain competitive.

This phenomenon has moved a step further recently in the potent alliance made between good environmental practice and consumer power—an alliance encouraged by the fact that as manufacturing techniques become increasingly standardized and the difference between competing products becomes increasingly marginal, the consumer's purchase tends to be won by the attractiveness of the packaging or the skill of the advertising copy writer rather than the technical excellence of the product itself. Consumers prefer a product whose manufacturer sends a message they believe and believe in.

We have reached the point in history where it is difficult and almost meaningless to identify the nationality of many of our products. I really don't know when I order a new Ford Motor car whether I am buying something that is British, Japanese or European. In fact, it probably depends on the model I select. I am, however, reasonably clear that I am not buying something American, in spite of the fact that the ultimate holding company headquarters is in Detroit.

In his book, *The Borderless World*, Kenichi Ohmae develops the concept of the equidistant manager. This person's task is to sit above local and national markets, rather than in any one of them, to see how the product in question can be adapted to the needs and traditions of the particular society he wishes to penetrate. Ohmae cites the example of Coca-Cola, which amazingly has seventy percent of the soft drinks market in Japan. This was achieved by carefully establishing a sales and distribution network appropriate to the ethos and expectations of Japanese culture. In other words, the multinational corporation learns how to work with and within its desired market and not simply to force entry on the basis of what worked in its home economy. It seeks to ally itself to the community in which it is operating. This is beginning to happen on a very large scale in Britain as Japanese companies are sensing an enthusiastic welcome for their new factories. The British people know that even though much of the companies' capital may be owned in Japan, this development is essentially beneficial to the community, for a basically good corporate citizen, a Japanese one, is coming to dwell among them.

At a very different level, the heated debate in Britain carried on largely within the Conservative Party about the extent and depth of British participation in European institutional life seems to have left the business community absolutely cold. It is as though business leaders, along with almost all young people in our country, know intuitively that this is yesterday's preoccupation. In practice, the whole of Europe is already part of their domestic market, or if it is not, they know it should be. They begin to have eyes that can take in the entire world, just as young people, more or less able to travel the globe without hindrance, see national borders as increasingly irrelevant. Kenichi Ohmae illustrates the extraordinary scale of the latter change with the amazing fact that nearly ninety percent of all Japanese honeymooners spend this important moment in their lives overseas.

There is another strand in the rapid change affecting international business. Unlike the United States, post-war political thinking in Britain was dominated by the idea of the welfare state. People thought that a more just society would be created by the intervention of the state; hence this was an area in which business had no place. According to this view, commerce should create wealth, maximize earnings per share, and leave the rest to government. As these halcyon and perhaps simplistic notions gave way in the 1970s to anxiety about government's ability to deliver the kind of education, health and welfare that had been promised, strains began to surface. These culminated in a spate of very ugly inner-city riots in 1981 and again in 1985. Suddenly business knew that if it sat by and did nothing, its very license to operate might be threatened.

Unlike the United States, where distant disturbances in the Watts area of Los Angeles could be virtually ignored in Columbus, Ohio, my country is so small that trouble in the Brixton area of London meant trouble across the whole nation. It followed from this fact that business could no longer "leave it to government," and the whole thrust for involvement by business, not just in generating an adequate return to shareholders but in playing a key role in insuring the viability of local communities, its marketplace, was born. Business leaders began to see the truth of the point make by the Prince of Wales at Davos: "Business can only succeed in a sustainable environment. Illiterate, poorly trained, poorly housed, resentful communities, deprived of a sense of belonging or of roots, provide a poor workforce and an uncertain market."

The creative role of business

All of this has brought us to a new era. Business now steps firmly upon the stage claiming a say in the way the totality is managed, not just the fragment of creation owing allegiance to the shareholders. It claims a say and involvement, a partnership, but not exclusivity. It wants not a takeover but a share in the processes that will decide the future shape of society. Furthermore, business is engaged in this drama for the long term and cannot escape. If it is in the long-term interest of all the constituent parts of business, especially of its shareholders, to care about the viability of the marketplace, business will never be able to stop caring.

This realization is fresh and growing rapidly, and the wise international company is beginning to learn how to manage this new power and responsibility. The learning curve has to be very fast indeed, though there is no map to follow, just a few sign posts. I well remember visiting a Standard Oil office in Chicago in the mid-1980s and being intrigued to discover just how much of its community budget was being applied toward inner-city projects. The director in charge vehemently denied my suggestion that this was enlightened philanthropy. He patiently explained that the only way in which the local market for gasoline could be expanded was through increasing the number of car owners. The Black community income per capita was extremely low; hence Standard was involved in an investment program to change this and thus to increase its market share. For me this was the first sighting of a new and powerful engine for social justice.

Multinational corporations like IBM, British Gas, ARCO, Grand Metropolitan, and a host more have gradually been feeling their way into this new ground and developing a resilient business case for their growing involvement. Grand Metropolitan, for example, goes so far as to say that "empowerment" is a good definition of the way in which they run their own business. In their language, they delegate to employees the capacity to succeed, giving people the tools to do their job and the freedom to get on with it. They apply the same concept to much of their community involvement. Our aim, they say, is to focus our efforts and resources on giving the less privileged members of society the same opportunity to compete and to win that we extend to our own employees. In other words, we empower them. It is no accident, therefore, that many of Grand Metropolitan's community programs concentrate on the less privileged. If they neglect this group, they contribute to the development of an underclass with little or no purchasing power for their own products.

Moreover, such corporations know that if they make a mistake in one corner of the globe, it will reverberate immediately, undermining consumer confidence worldwide. The multinational that tries out dangerous products on rural African communities will reap an increasingly rapid backlash against all their products in the supermarkets of Columbus.

Bitter experience has taught many British companies that they cannot expect to call the shots in this new game. Involvement with local communities, if it is to endure, requires a new form of listening and partnership. The solutions to community problems and the meeting of community aspirations can no longer be imposed from the outside. Already I sense that business understands this with greater clarity than government. The 1980s in Britain have seen the creation of a whole range of new mediating structures. It seems as though business and the local community cannot yet deal directly with each other; they need first to create some kind of half-way house where they can meet, explore, and then plan together on level terms. It is here that I sense a point of contact with liberation theology.

The meeting of business and religion

Thanks to the worldwide attention being devoted during this Columbus quincentennial year to the colonial era and all its terrible shortcomings, that period is increasingly seen as one of theological as well as social violence. The imposition of Western Christianity upon the Southern world, with the colonial leaders' explicit view that slavery was acceptable as long as the slaves could be forced into baptism and instructed in the Christian religion, is yielding an inescapable backlash. Now that much of the Christian churches' vitality is emerging from those historically oppressed cultures, it is difficult to imagine initiative swinging back to the powerful European sectors. This shift is laying bare the gap between Western Christendom's power politics and the gospel. Thanks to the insights of liberation theology, we are realizing afresh that the poor and oppressed are especially responsive to and knowledgeable about the gospel message. They must be taken seriously by those of us in positions of power; their chains must be broken, their wounds healed, their voices heard.

As one living in Britain today, I concur with those who believe the church now draws its dynamism largely from its attention to disadvantaged peoples around the world. So, too, I believe it is in the direct interest of international corporations to hear, empower and thus set free from poverty and injustice those who will increasingly become its consumers as the planet shrinks. This means that surely there is potential for creative cooperation between religious leaders who are attentive to the poor and corporate leaders who guide the world of business. Indeed, I suggest that however strange this may sound, the future of each is inextricably bound up with the other.

I want to conclude by saying that those of us who are interested in ethics and theology now have a remarkable new opportunity and responsibility. The people who lead businesses and invest in them are infinitely influenceable. The moment is ripe to launch a campaign that encourages a whole new level of social responsibility on the part of business and that recognizes Fortune 500 companies as the most appropriate vehicle for positive social change globally.

Such a campaign might have five starting points. First is the understanding that corporate community involvement (which is my British language) and the ethics of international business (which is your North American language) are effectively the same thing. Good behavior within a business has its reverse or flip side in the power and potential of business to influence positively the development of the whole world. The second starting point is the fact that companies will have to earn their freedom to operate from local communities and from consumers. This will not stop; it will endure. The third point is that in a borderless world the poor will demand social justice and, as we are seeing in South Africa, they will ultimately be heard. The fourth point is that by listening to the poor, corporations will find the way to make their contribution to a more just world. Finally, business will need to move beyond an excessively short term view of its own potential. This will mean, as we are beginning to see in Britain, that the governing boards of corporations must be responsive not just to shareholder power but to consumer power and to stakeholders of all sorts.

I believe that international business today is the only vehicle we have to create positive and rapid social change, and that world religions are ideally placed to influence and pressure them. Business does not need lecturing from the outside. It needs consumer pressure to keep it on its toes, but it also needs wise and trusted counselors who will help it recognize and respond to the fact that building up the people who are its marketplace is in its own self-interest. I hope that as leaders from business, religion and academia come together in gatherings like this one, we shall discover a path forward that lets us combine our separate strands and establish a way of putting sustained and encouraging pressure on business to transform so much of the world that so badly needs it.

I believe also that the credit due to business is very real and that those of us from outside the business community have an important role to play in singing the praise of what business is already doing. Thus we can encourage it in its new role of being, perhaps, the peacemaker of the third millennium.

3

Ethics in Business—A European Approach

Wilfried Guth

A "crisis of progress"

From the writings of Alexander von Humboldt we know how deeply the first European to set foot on the North American continent was impressed by its overwhelming natural beauty. Von Humboldt tells us that Christopher Columbus was fascinated by "the beauty of this new land." Five hundred years later, as we approach it by plane, this land of economic wealth provokes very different observations. The picture is one of affluence, technology and almost total organization. Life is shaped by business achievements, no longer by the cycles of nature. We are not content as people were in earlier times to discover nature; we want to dominate it. But it is exactly this nature that points out to us more and more clearly the limits of our business dealings if they are directed solely toward economic growth and increased wealth.

After Columbus' fascination with the beauties of nature, later generations did not follow up with the corresponding attention and care; on the contrary, in many areas uncontrolled exploitation became established. Recently, however, we have become aware of the alarming consequences of our actions. The first publications of the Club of Rome were important in this context. Though largely ignored at the time (all the more so as their basic philosophy was hostile to growth and some of their extrapolations and prognoses proved to be over-pessimistic), these works focused attention on the environmental problem. In some countries the "green" parties, while otherwise often misguided and even destructive, also helped to raise public awareness. Today there is no doubt that unchecked technological progress and excessive quantitative growth would upset

P.M. Minus (ed.), *The Ethics of Business in a Global Economy.*

the delicate balance of nature, causing considerable suffering to us and even more to later generations.

In the main, therefore, ecological problems have led us to perceive a "crisis of progress," even though similar symptoms of crisis are evident elsewhere. And it is precisely this "crisis of progress" that underlies our present concern with "ethics in business." Few people today will dispute the claim that growth and the pursuit of profit, though still decisively important for any private enterprise, cannot be the sole guidelines for entrepreneurial activity, let alone the sole criteria for measuring entrepreneurial success. Other basic human values must also be brought into such an assessment. We could paraphrase a statement from the Bible: "For what shall it profit a man, if he shall gain outstanding growth, the highest affluence, and the greatest profit, and yet he damages his natural environment and thereby also his human substance?"

The ethics discussion now is in full swing in the United States, Europe and Japan. It has entered the universities, some of which have created business ethics professorships, and it is a popular subject at many symposia and conferences. You could even say that business ethics has become the fashion and that anyone who does not join in is behind the times.

Given the fact that just following fashions is not very dignified, you might think me a little skeptical or sarcastic about this conference! On the contrary, because this subject is usually dealt with too superficially and the professing of business ethics often threatens to deteriorate into mere lip service (a well-known and highly responsible Swiss manager recently exclaimed, "I can't hear the word 'ethics' any more!"), I think it is extremely important to go into greater depth here and discuss openly where the "ethical weaknesses," the perils or temptations in our entrepreneurial activity, lie and what ethical standards we should apply when assessing our business conduct. So it is a particular pleasure for me to participate in this conference as a European, and it is also a special honor to dedicate my remarks, at the request of the conference organizers, to the memory of Alfred Herrhausen, my friend and colleague at the Deutsche Bank, who was murdered in 1989 by deluded terrorists, and whose life and business conduct were guided by the highest ethical principles.

The Western ethical tradition and economics

Concern with ethical questions is, of course, as old as Western history; ethics has always been a central theme of philosophy and Christian moral theory, and it still is today. Other religions have their own ethical standards, which in a number of ways differ from Christian tenets. In our Western culture, ethics began with Plato. Aristotle raised it to an independent philosophical discipline alongside logic and physics. Its object was the question of the greatest good, the right measure from which rational and virtuous action would ensue. St. Thomas Aquinas took these ancient sources as the basis for his philosophical-theological ethics, which has remained a powerful intellectual force.

For the Christian churches, the concept of justice has always been at the center of moral thinking. Working from the basic postulate of a divine and worldly order, two economic phenomena appear at the center of critical attention: price and interest. Accordingly, entrepreneurial activity is considered necessary in order to satisfy people's basic material needs, which, in turn, are prerequisites for attaining spiritual and intellectual goals of a higher order. At the same time, though, profit-oriented enterprise or "usury" is deemed reprehensible, because it is considered an end in itself.

This is neither the time nor the place to pursue the theological and historical connection between economic and ethical questions over the centuries. Let it suffice to point out the almost paradoxical reversal of the Christian propositions I have just mentioned that developed in the Puritan-Calvinistic view, according to which profit-oriented entrepreneurial activity, coupled with an ascetic life-style, is pleasing to God. In his essay *The Protestant Ethic and the Spirit of Capitalism*, Max Weber, the well-known German sociologist, cited this combination (pursued not for hedonistic profit consumption but for saving, i.e., capital formation) as the driving force behind modern capitalism, a view also put forward in R.H. Tawney's famous work, *Religion and the Rise of Capitalism*. I should mention parenthetically that this business philosophy does not seem to be too dissimilar to the Buddhistic roots of the Japanese economic success.

I have briefly sketched this historical background in order to show, on the one hand, that the present-day discussion of ethics in business, notwithstanding the differences in accent, has significant historical precedent, and also to ask, on the other, whether the last fifty years have not seen a certain lack of self-critical ethical reflection on the business practice (and partly also on the theory) of our very successful capitalist system.

Looking back to the origins of Western classical liberalism, to thinkers like Montesquieu, David Hume and John Stuart Mill, one sees that the situation then was entirely different from our own. Like them, Adam Smith dealt with moral-philosophical questions and wrote his *Theory of Moral Sentiments* before he wrote his chief work, *The Wealth of Nations*, now considered the Bible of our liberal system, although it is often still misunderstood as the glorification of egoistic pursuit of personal advantage. Today, by contrast, we get the impression that this kind of parallel occupation with both ethics and economics has been largely foreign to more recent theorists and practitioners of our economy. Scholars in the two fields have had little to do with one another. This applies in particular to the study of business management, whose conceptual framework has no place for ethical considerations. Accordingly, many people have regarded business enterprises and banks as entities committed solely to material aims. And, indeed, with increasing secularization and the associated decline of Christian moral values, materialistic thinking has gained the upper hand in many areas.

So it can hardly surprise us that, right up into recent times, the Roman Catholic Church in particular has felt called upon to point its finger at the weaknesses of the capitalist system, though without a constructive proposal of practicable remedies. However, with its social theory it has succeeded in establishing the good of all participants in the economic process as the ultimate goal of all business activity.

Nor can it astonish us that many people recently in Eastern Germany and Eastern Europe, for all the joy of liberation after the dramatic upheaval there, have asked uneasily whether the "victorious" capitalist system should really be affirmed and welcomed on all points. Even in the West, especially among young people, there is growing doubt about whether the affluent society (which tends to be an "elbow society") can be the ultimate goal of the industrial nations, especially as there is still deep poverty in many parts of the world. These doubts partly explain why people turn to religions and cults in search of life's purpose.

The general shift in values toward responsiveness to post-material needs, as articulated in the call for more ecological sensitivity and greater responsibility for the socially disadvantaged, has come, understandably enough, at a time when the material aspects of life are no longer a problem for most people. There is something like a longing for a new ethic. Catastrophes all over the world have played a part in this as well: Exxon Valdez, Sandoz, Seveso and Chernobyl, to name just a few, although we must of course distinguish between human error, carelessness and irresponsible behavior in these events. And so people's attention turns increasingly to those who are responsible for corporate decisions and to the economic system whose prominent representatives are the entrepreneurs.

Ethics and the free market system

Our topic here is *ethics in business*. But my remarks so far have shown that the economic system in which businesses must operate stands on trial. How can businesses act ethically, one might ask, if ethical principles have no place in their economic system? As for the communist or centrally planned socialist system, we need no longer spend time on the subject. Its economic failure is just as evident as its complete disregard for the basic ethical values of freedom and human dignity.

But what about our system, practiced in most parts of the world today, which I will refer to as "capitalist" for simplicity's sake, even if I do not feel completely comfortable with the use of this term, which is so often misunderstood and misinterpreted. As a German, it does not come naturally to me anyway, for we Germans usually speak of "social market economy"—*Soziale Marktwirtschaft*. But that term is not used internationally, partly because (as we shall see) of its different content.

If we set these terminological matters aside for now, the first question to be clarified is this: By what ethical criteria are the economic systems—and later on, corporate business policies—to be measured? I think that part of our current uncertainty starts right here. Naturally, all governments and businesses claim to function ethically (who would say otherwise?), yet such assertions are of little value if they do not stand the test of concrete standards.

It is difficult to determine the priority among basic ethical postulates; the following should be understood as merely a list, without any attempt to rank its parts:

- *preserving freedom and human dignity, democratic order, rule of law*
- *safeguarding peace*
- *protecting the environment*
- *maintaining solidarity with the socially weak, both nationally and internationally.*

I believe we can say that our free market system, like no other, upholds and fulfills these ethical requirements to a high degree. Happily, people have stopped the search for a "third way" between free markets and the socialist centrally planned economy. Of course, our system, which has proven itself so overwhelmingly, can and should be improved just like any human institution. Recognize, however, that ethical "misconduct," which provokes justified criticism, is usually the fault of the individual responsible and not of the system.

As we all know, the central weakness of our system has been the lack of regard for ecological issues. But a far-reaching correctional process is under way worldwide, with varying intensity from country to country. In fact, in some government programs one can even say that ecology is being overemphasized at the expense of the economy. In some instances (here I think of my own country) application and approval procedures for new pharmaceutical products have become so complicated and cumbersome that whole research units have been moved to the United States. But aside from this kind of exaggeration, some very reasonable steps have been taken to promote environment-friendly conduct conforming with market principles, e.g., by tax incentives or penalties. And at the same time the business sector has widely begun to accept its responsibility for the environment, declaring its support for the target of "sustainable development" as formulated by the Brundtland Commission.

In opposition to the securing of peace, there continues to be the exporting of weapons and matériel that can be used for military purposes in areas outside of NATO, even in the face of general disarmament and the end of the East-West conflict. This is certainly no chapter of glory for our system, as events in Libya and the Gulf War have shown all too clearly. But here, too, governments are taking remedial measures, even if this is easier said than done without excessive bureaucratic controls and regimentation. The task is made all the more difficult by the fact that many products can be put to both military and civilian uses. It is gratifying to note that more and more firms have become aware of their responsibility in this field and have imposed voluntary limits on themselves.

With respect to supporting the poor in one's own country and thus expressing the social component of our free enterprise system, things vary greatly throughout the world. I hope I am not stepping on my hosts' toes by voicing the opinion that this task has not been given the attention it deserves in recent years in the United States and the United Kingdom. This has certainly not resulted from disregard for the problems of the poor, but from the ideology that "the world only belongs to the fit," which has been a powerful force in American history. This view has been coupled with too heavy a reliance on the charity of private individuals who could afford to be generous. In Great Britain, Prime Minister Major is trying to correct this view, for which Margaret Thatcher was a staunch advocate.

At the other end of the scale are the nations that have overshot the welfare idea and thus exercised the redistribution of income on a grand scale, thereby often detracting from private initiative and personal responsibility; let me name Sweden as an example.

In the "golden middle" (I hope you excuse this praise of my own country) stands the social market economy as introduced by Ludwig Erhard and Alfred Müller-Armack. This is a system in which social concerns and free competition have been successfully combined for over four decades. It is more than an economic set of rules; it is an intellectual concept. As a side note, I am pleased that Pope John Paul II expressly recognized this system in his last encyclical. In this connection I cannot emphasize enough how important it is in my opinion today for the Western world, which is being observed so attentively by Eastern Europe and rather hostilely by the Islamic world, to develop and foster the humane values of our economic order—the values beyond supply and demand, as Wilhelm Röpke called them.

Now a word about worldwide social politics and aid for the peoples of the less developed world. Much has been done by the industrial nations and some improvement has been achieved, but we all know that it is not nearly enough. Also, we know that some types of official economic aid to developing countries were misdirected. At any rate, the North-South gap has hardly been reduced, and now that the East-West conflict is over, the North-South divide is threatening to become the greatest source of conflict for the world economy and world politics. This fact places demands on our system, and it tests the willingness to sacrifice on the part of every individual, even if we must emphasize again and again that such assistance can and should be only a matter of "help for self-help."

The ethical obligation of management

I have looked at the economic system in such detail because businesses are an integral part of it and their ethical (or unethical) conduct is largely shaped by the economic order in which they operate. Let me now turn to the businesses themselves or, more correctly, to the entrepreneurs, because they alone determine their companies' policies. A company as an institution has no ethical quality. There is no such thing as an "unethical business," there are only businesses that are unethically managed. Ethical conduct must be clearly visible to all staff members in the behavior of management. Corporate ethics, like other ethics, is the outcome of individual actions. Therefore, company ethics is strongly linked to personal ethics.

So where does the ethical obligation of management lie within the framework prescribed by the free market economic system and the democratic political order? Is it not enough to work within this order to achieve general affluence and high employment levels by means of intelligent and competent business dealings and corresponding profits? In this sense I somewhat provokingly spoke on another occasion of the "ethics of profit-seeking." In fact, profit is the central yardstick by which businesses and managements are measured, and rightly so. It goes without saying that this corporate achievement loses its claim to ethical standing if obtained by dishonest means, such as corruption or bribery.

The "ethics of profit-seeking" also includes the essential obligation to treat staff members fairly and with respect for their dignity. In contrast to the tenets of Manchester capitalism, business success can hardly be achieved today without proper employee motivation and without proper attention to such matters as dismantling hierarchies, holding open talks with employees, maintaining teamwork, and much more.

And yet this answer is not enough. Management's list of values must be longer, going on to encompass areas outside the confines of the company. Environmental protection is one of these key areas I would like to look at more closely. Despite governments' sensitivity to ecological matters, it is neither imaginable nor desirable that businesses should be freed from all decisions in this field by a network of regulations. The state and the business community must share this responsibility and, above all, they must work together. What's more, forward-looking solutions to many environmental problems can never be found without the creative and innovative participation of industry. This is especially well demonstrated by the chemical and pharmaceutical sectors. We today have a whole set of state regulations for the environmentally safe conduct of industry and for the production and sale of pharmaceuticals. But these regulations cannot cover everything and, most importantly, they can never be fully current, because research and development will always be far ahead of the authorities' knowledge and understanding.

Such situations call for corporate ethics, and here managers must decide on their own responsibility, according to their best knowledge and belief. In so doing, they cannot take refuge in any generally binding guidelines or written codes of business ethics, because no established guidelines of a general character exist, and it is hard to imagine that they will ever exist, no matter how much academic attention is given to the subject. Many enterprises have developed constructive procedures for preparing and examining company decisions with a view to their ethical implications. There are in-house corporate codes of conduct and managers responsible solely for environmental matters. Ecological appraisals are carried out and panels have been created in which businessmen, scientists and others examine the issues. Nonetheless, the final decision has to be made by the CEO or the management board.

Here we come to the core of the problem, for this decision is often very difficult. It is difficult since the ethical postulates, such as forgoing the production or sale of a particular product because of its possibly damaging effect on the environment or on people, often conflict with the necessity for profit, which must be the pivot for every enterprise and for our economic system. Furthermore, against the background of national and especially international competition, there is no guarantee that competitors will display the same ethical restraint. An ethically motivated decision might, therefore, lead to serious losses in market share, which the manager would have to account for to his stockholders.

For this reason, institutions like the International Chamber of Commerce work intensely to bring national environmental regulations into line all over the world, so that a level playing field is ensured among competitors. A document issued by the ICC states that "environmental regulations, and measures that have as their justification environmental protection, should be devised to minimize distortions of international trade and investment flows and to avoid the creation of trade barriers." This statement also reflects the concern, recently being looked into primarily by GATT, that environmental demands may in truth only be veiled protectionist endeavors. This conference can and should encourage the worldwide acceptance of ecological principles, but we certainly have still got a long way to go on this important issue.

It is hardly necessary to explain that those concerned about corporate ethics are faced with completely different problems in the individual branches of business. For example, the ethics of commercial and investment banking is a very special field, but it would take too long to go into that in any detail. In recent years there has been no lack of offenses against ethical principles here, such as laundering of money, financing illegal businesses, using insider knowledge, and the like. In these fast-moving times of yuppies and quick profits, ethical standards have begun to crumble in the financial world. Buy-out transactions with the sole purpose of asset-stripping must also be considered as an offense against ethical business conduct. It is true in banking as well that supervisory regulations and internal control mechanisms, as necessary as they are, cannot cover all relevant matters; so, here again, the ethical conscience of the individual must come into play

Ethical questions of a different sort arise for the media or for advertising in our demanding society, which seems to acknowledge almost no limits. One can wonder whether everything that is done to achieve higher circulations, viewer ratings or sales figures is compatible with ethical principles, and even more with a sense of responsibility toward young people. It is above all a question of truth and human dignity. This applies particularly to television networks and stations that resort to sensationalist reporting in the fight for economic advantage. But we must bear in mind that consumers create demand through their buying behavior, and to this extent they also can exert a regulating influence.

Hopefully, ethical behavior on the part of companies will be increasingly accepted and rewarded by society and the marketplace, as is already the case today, for example, with environmentally safe products. Thus, research and development with this goal in mind can be worthwhile and produce a competitive advantage. But, of course, if such policies lead to profit optimization no ethical problem is involved any longer.

In my opinion, for a business leader to act ethically means perceiving and bearing responsibility for the consequences of one's decisions and deeds with respect to society, even if this means sacrificing short-term profits. Hardly anyone has expressed this better than Alfred Herrhausen. His words are instructive: "Our economic and social order are in need of a new synthesis of freedom and commitment, of rights and obligations. Not as deontological ethics, which seeks the absolute, but rather as responsibility ethics that consider the consequences of an action in full knowledge of the situation at hand."

To "consider the consequences" means nothing more than forgoing conduct that runs counter to the basic ethical goals I have mentioned, and to do so of one's own free will. This sort of ethical behavior only pertains to areas not regulated by the state. No one can claim that he is acting ethically by merely observing environmental regulations or government bans on exporting weapons. Likewise, not following them is not only unethical, it is criminal. Ethics and personal responsibility are inseparably connected! The philosopher Hans Jonas describes this in a most impressive manner in his major work, *The Principle of Responsibility*.

Remembering the personality of Alfred Herrhausen takes us to another aspect of the subject of personal ethics. If in the final analysis the ethics of business is nothing other than the ethical sense of responsibility of the manager or the management board, then it is clear that their life-style and attitude toward society must be taken into consideration. Because of his commitment to the *res publica*, his personal modesty, and his friendly and unassuming manner in dealing with colleagues and employees (he often had a beer with his bodyguards), Herrhausen was a manager to whom respect and sympathy flowed. He was convincing and credible as a human being; he set a shining example. It is scarcely necessary to mention that the opposite behavior among managers—such things as an excessively luxurious life-style, arrogance, poor treatment of employees, tax fraud or political disinterest—are hardly likely to convince the public that these very same people make ethically sound decisions in their capacity as company managers.

Six conclusions

I will now attempt to formulate a few conclusions.

1. The discussion about ethical business now under way is good and useful; it was neglected for much too long. Such discussion constitutes a meaningful and necessary correlate and corrective to "pure" economic theory and business management, and it helps to increase entrepreneurial awareness of these questions in business practice. But this latter goal cannot be achieved unless the ideas and impulses come from the companies that have the practical experience. Academic considerations not building on practical experience run the risk of establishing abstract principles that end up being non-committal, because they are not relevant to real decision-making situations. This topic does not lend itself to fruitful discussion unless based on concrete case studies (such as have been prepared for this conference). And because of the diverse nature of ethical problems in different industries—chemicals, power plant construction, defense, banking, etc.—any attempt to establish universally valid rules or theories is doomed to fail.

2. Ethical business practice unfolds within the economic system created by government, which must establish a clear framework of regulations for operating the social security system, for protecting the environment, for assuring the soundness of the banking system, for preventing the export of weapons, etc., in line with its responsibility to all citizens, including future generations. These regulations are not meant to exempt companies from ethical considerations and decisions, which would be impossible anyway. But it is one of the obligations of the state to provide uniform conditions for fair competition in the marketplace. The more successfully this is done, the sooner ethically-minded companies can gain market advantages based on broad public acceptance.

3. In many cases, environmental issues are just as global in their scope as economic ones. So national regulations can hardly

come up with satisfactory solutions to such issues. That is why largely uniform global environmental standards would be such a good thing. First steps in this direction have been taken, but we can not expect this process to continue smoothly and on a broad front. What is conceivable, however, is the formulation of international codes for certain business sectors that, though not enforceable, could serve as a kind of guideline for entrepreneurial decisions; they could cover technical norms, questions of security and the like. Europe is moving toward a much more closely knit network of uniform ecological standards, with the result that competitive distortions stemming from differing national environmental legislation should gradually disappear.

Things are different with respect to the much wider postulate of a global set of ethics in a broad philosophical-moralistic sense. Such a development would be logically and morally justified, for ethical values should apply in the same way to all human beings. Nonetheless, this idea is probably rather utopian, because differences in religion, culture and tradition are not easy to overcome. That does not mean that all those actively engaged in international business should not treat each other according to the rules of courtesy, fairness and truthfulness, as their sense of honor and conscience dictates.

4. Companies would be well advised to take the ethics discussion seriously and to make sure that the subject receives attention at all levels of their hierarchy. In other words, corporate culture should have strong ethical accents. Companies should make their ecological stance known to the public, through "environmental audits," for example. They must be willing to forgo some of their short-term profits in favor of important, long-term ethical goals and not regard this as a "sin" against the market economy. Today the idea of *optimizing* profits, in contrast to *maximizing* them, must also take environmental requirements into account.

On the other hand, we must not fall for arguments that purport to raise ethical sensibilities but in fact are just poorly veiled ideological maneuvers. In Germany I could name in this connection the exaggerated debate on nuclear energy, the escalating hostility to cars, and the unconditional pacifism that is even willing to forfeit freedom itself. It should also be said that companies or banks are not charitable establishments able to give their poorer customers price reductions or provide cheaper credit. Likewise, economic aid to developing countries is no task for private companies. On the other hand, however, it reflects well on companies, as part of society, to donate a certain portion of their profits to charities, schools or other cultural institutions.

5. All in all, companies in the West can face the discussion of ethics without a guilty conscience or self-accusation. The "mishaps" that occurred in recent years were partly the result of unforeseeable technical developments that have been remedied. In other cases, managers indeed failed to act responsibly and have been punished. What is most important is the fact that a gradual learning process is under way in this whole field in both business and the academic world.

6. The ethics debate was triggered largely by technical progress. In turn, it has resulted in technical corrective measures and new research. The bottom line, though, is the role and responsibility of the individual in the economic decision-making process. Ethics in business can not be dealt with in isolation from personal integrity, overall values and moral-philosophical questions. As Alfred Herrhausen put it: "We must say what we think, do what we say, and be what we do."

4

The Ethics of Business—An Asian Approach

Hiroyuki Yoshino

The Honda experience

There is considerable discussion going on in Japan today about the social responsibility of business. This has been stimulated partly by the recent securities scandals and the collapse of what is called the "bubble economy." Another important discussion now under way in Japan is directed to major environmental issues such as global warming, ozone layer destruction, and recycling, in addition to more traditional issues like air, water and noise pollution.

Because my four years of living and working in the United States have kept me from being up-to-date about such discussions among Japanese executives, I shall concentrate instead on other areas in which I am directly involved, especially the current consideration of ethical business practice within the Honda Motor Company, both in Japan and in the U.S.

At the beginning of 1992, Honda issued a document entitled "The Honda Philosophy." For Honda management associates worldwide, this statement was the result of three years of discussions and documentation among key associates in different countries. Our goal was to re-examine and reorganize Honda's basic approach to business in ways that can be shared among all key associates worldwide into the twenty-first century.

Honda is now in its forty-fourth year and has enjoyed remarkable growth that no one even within the corporation could have foreseen. Consolidated annual revenue now amounts to about 30 billion dollars, with 68 plants in 37 countries outside of Japan. Honda has a total of 87,000 employees worldwide. Half of these are

P.M. Minus (ed.), *The Ethics of Business in a Global Economy*.

Japanese and half are non-Japanese, with the latter expected to increase from now on.

We believe the key to Honda's growth worldwide lies in the philosophies and genius of our founders, Mr. Soichiro Honda and Mr. Takeo Fujisawa, both of whom passed away in recent years—Mr. Fujisawa in December 1988, and Mr. Honda in August 1991. The current top management team of Honda thus is the fourth and last generation to be taught their philosophies directly by our founders. It is our responsibility to organize these philosophies and basic concepts, reflecting the global nature of our business and the progress of technology. It is also our responsibility to share these philosophies with all Honda associates worldwide in order to establish a common corporate culture and transfer it to coming generations.

Our corporate philosophy has much to say about the many issues of ethical business, for they came up repeatedly during our recent discussions of company policy and reorganization. It became apparent during this process that people of different nationalities or experience sometimes have a different approach to ethical issues. Yet, there also were many things we have in common, including the Honda Philosophy.

The Honda Philosophy starts with respect for the individual, and it causes us to look both externally and internally.

At Honda of America Manufacturing, we currently employ more than 10,000 associates at four plants in west central Ohio. These associates have many unique abilities but one common responsibility—to know their customers and exceed their expectations. This means being responsible not only to the customers who purchase a Honda product, but also to our *internal customers*—the thousands of other Honda associates who depend on the quality of each person's work to do *their* work with quality and value added. To perform this job well, we must think about how our job affects others. We must think about how we treat each other.

At Honda of America, this responsibility starts with providing a safe and comfortable working environment for all associates. We also encourage associates to be involved, to speak up and contribute ideas and suggestions. Thus, it is our responsibility to create fair and equal opportunities for associates' involvement, development and advancement. This is business ethics at the shop-floor level.

"Three joys" plus one

Another important concept to Honda is "The Three Joys." We believe that each person working in our company, or coming in touch with our company, directly or through our products, should share a sense of joy through that experience. This responsibility is expressed in what we call "The Three Joys." Our goal is to provide joy for those who buy our products, sell our products and produce our products. We have often discussed whether we should add a fourth joy—the joy of contributing to the society or the community in which we do business. This latter concept actually has been an implicit part of Honda for a long time, although it has not been expressed as explicitly as the other ones. We believe we *must* be a contributing part of any society where Honda is present.

This sense of ethical business and responsibility to our communities comes directly from the top. Honda Motor's president, Mr. Kawamoto, recently said to associates at Honda of America: "Right now we face challenges that will test our company's culture. It is our responsibility to make a positive contribution to society."

This concern has been evident for many years at Honda. As our motorcycle business became successful and motorcycles grew to be a very popular means of transportation, motorcycle accidents also increased. As early as 1970, Honda established the Safe Driving Promotion Center within our company to develop education and training programs for safer driving. Honda Motor or our distributors now operate a total of seventeen traffic education schools or motorcycle rider education centers in the world—five in Japan, five in the United States and seven in six other countries. To date, more than one million people have participated in our safety promotion programs, including practical rider education training. Hundreds of thousands of people are now trained worldwide each year, including police officers for traffic control.

In 1974, when motor vehicle use in Japan began to increase dramatically and negative side effects were becoming apparent, Honda established the International Association of Traffic and Safety Sciences in an effort to realize a better traffic society. Members of the Association are business leaders, engineers, scientists, psychologists, professors, government officials, lawyers, journalists, artists and novelists worldwide. The Association organizes international symposia, conducts research activities, develops information systems, and makes grants and awards. But the major focus is on the creation of a more desirable role for transportation in society and the achievement of a harmonious balance between technology and humanity.

Realizing that science and technology are playing an increasingly important role in society, Honda Motor established the Honda Foundation in December 1977. The objective of the Foundation is to contribute to the creation of a humane civilization through establishing an "eco-technology," which is a compound word combining "ecology" and "technology." Our concern is that technology should aim at harmony with the overall environment of human activities rather than exist merely to increase efficiency or profit. To realize the goal of eco-technology, the Honda Foundation developed an international symposium named "The Discoveries." So far, ten of these symposia have been held, including one here in Columbus in May 1982. Also, a special recognition called the Honda Prize is awarded annually to an individual or an organization for distinguished achievement in the field of eco-technology.

With these and other examples as background, we have continued to discuss the incorporation of a fourth joy into our Honda Philosophy.

Practical ethical questions

Honda leaders have approached the subject of ethics in business by discussing practical aspects of our business in order to develop actual guidelines which could be used on a global basis. One of the guidelines we have discussed says that Honda should stick to the mainline of its business, which is manufacturing, and not try to find some other way of making money. An implication of this is to prohibit investment or profiteering in such speculative areas as foreign currency exchange, the stock market, land investment or mergers and acquisitions. Even if such a speculative transaction were successful, Honda believes that it would undermine the ethics of associates who are required day in and day out to improve quality and cost in every detail on the plant floor, thus putting the very existence of the company at risk.

I might note that because of this prohibition, it was no surprise to us that Honda was *not* mentioned several months ago in

Japan when a long list of company names was announced in conjunction with the securities scandals.

This reminds me of the recent controversy associated with GM's restructuring plan and President Bush's visit to Japan in January 1992. We have read and heard much discussion about the compensation of corporate executives and the relationship of management responsibility to employee sacrifice in cases of restructuring or plant closing. In Japan, it is common sense that management compensation is reduced first or management change is required before employees are laid off. This is an example of how ethics in business can be different from one country to another, although it may be just a difference of management style.

Another example of management ethics, more directly related to business judgment in a global economy, is how to apply available technology to markets in countries with different levels of economic development. Honda now applies many advanced automotive technologies in developed countries: airbag and anti-lock braking systems for improved safety; exhaust emissions systems for air pollution control; various fuel economy improvement technologies for saving energy; and other environmental and health protection technologies such as recycling and use of non-CFC refrigerants or non-asbestos materials.

But legal requirements or standards are different from one country to another. Some are very strict, others less so; and some countries have none. Even within the United States, California has stricter auto emissions standards than other states.

In general, we do not apply *all* advanced systems to the products sold in *all* places. For example, the exhaust emissions system available to forty-nine states in the U.S. is less strict or controlled than the system for the California market. We do not believe that the quality of life should be better in certain places, nor do we think we should pollute more of the air in certain areas. Life is life. We value all life.

It is also true that many of those advanced technologies cost more—as much as hundreds of dollars more in each case—as compared to less advanced ones. These advanced technologies could cost a country billions of dollars more, depending upon the volume, which otherwise could be spent for more pressing or basic needs. So, which of these technologies should we apply in various countries?

We currently leave that decision to the local business leaders who know best what is necessary and what will be supported.

Ethically, however, there are questions. Should we be providing customers with choices regarding each of these technologies, even though production and distribution would become more complicated? Should a customer in Ohio be able to buy a California-spec emissions car, even at a higher price? Or, should we talk thoroughly with our business partners in developing countries about the details of these technologies, their cost-effectiveness and the cost-appropriate means of handling them? Should we provide our business partners with more options and choices, even if it means increasing costs?

As you can tell, such discussions can become very complicated. We do not yet have clear answers to these questions. That is why we want other viewpoints on such ethical questions.

You may wonder how we are doing in developing a statement about the fourth joy. The truth is, we are still working on it!

Honda's commitment to society is part of our basic company philosophy. When we realize the Three Joys, we should also be creating joy for society as a whole. Because of the industry we are in, we affect society in many ways. Some of these ways are positive—such as increasing personal mobility, giving the pride of owning a spirited and valued product, and providing employment opportunities. Some are negative—such as the environmental impact of our product. Further attention to social issues, especially safety and environmental concerns, is among the most pressing needs of our society.

In order to create joy for society and gain society's trust, we want to manufacture products and provide services that are needed, while at the same time minimizing any unwanted or negative effects of our products, services or other activities on society.

In all our business activities, we must seek to understand the meaning and importance of the Three Joys and their impact upon the larger society. As we respond to society's needs in this way, we believe that Honda's existence within society will be recognized and valued.

5

Ethics in Business—A North American Approach

Richard G. Capen, Jr.

Interdependence, values and ethics

My thirty-one years in the newspaper business have been capped by service since 1979 with Knight-Ridder. The company now has twenty-nine newspapers around the United States, but the fastest growing part of our business is the distribution of information electronically on-line to 130 countries. In this work I have been reminded repeatedly of how interdependent we have become around the world, not just in business but in many other areas as well.

I must admit that my overseas travels often have made me embarrassed and humiliated, for they have made me realize how arrogant we are in the United States. I have seen repeatedly that we Americans expect others to know all about us, but we do little to understand the culture, the politics and the values of others. Our practice contrasts sharply with a large bank in Tokyo, one of the top ten in the world, that has a program whereby every three years three hundred of their executives are moved to different parts of the world. This means that within a ten- or twenty-year period all their senior managers will speak three or four languages. You can imagine how effective they will be as international business leaders, for in addition to their linguistic ability, they will understand the values and the ways of doing business in a variety of cultures. Isn't there a lesson here for businesses in the United States?

As the world grows smaller and people inevitably learn more about the different ways of thinking and acting around the world, we all shall have occasion increasingly to ask about the values that people hold dear and the ethics that guide behavior. In fact, it will

P.M. Minus (ed.), *The Ethics of Business in a Global Economy.*

be those values and ethics that largely determine how people respond to the rapid changes that will continue to affect life on this planet for many years to come.

I believe that there are certain fundamental values that are important to us no matter what our language and no matter what our culture. Identifying those values is an important task, for as television commentator Ted Koppel has said, "there is harmony and inner peace to be found in following a moral compass that points in the same direction regardless of fashion or trend." We need that "harmony and inner peace" all the more today in the face of the economic hard times that have caught up with us. Here in the United States we have seen the collapse of entire industries and tremendous retrenchment. We have seen people going into business careers who have thought they were in a stable business where their careers would be solid and their companies would prosper. But then they have experienced the collapse of their bank, or their S & L, or their insurance company, and they have realized at fifty years of age that they have a very narrow specialty and now must totally redefine themselves. In this environment, one is pushed back to the basic personal values that identify who we are and what we most want for ourselves and our families.

There are millions of people around the world today who are being pushed by their circumstances to ask the same question about their basic values. I learned recently about a Moscow school teacher, a fifty-year-old woman, who admitted that "every teacher I ever had, every book I ever read, every Communist I ever heard, turned out to be a total fraud. I don't know who I am and I don't know what I should believe."

Ethical wills

In the face of the uncertainty about values and ethics that besets many people today, I think all of us can learn from what happened at another troubled time some fifty years ago. I recently visited a synagogue in the Jewish section of Warsaw that was absolutely devastated in World War II. Today, there are files in this synagogue containing what have been called "ethical wills." During the late 1930s and early 1940s, when the Jews in Warsaw realized that their possessions were being stripped from them and their relatives were being taken away by the Nazis, they saw that they must leave behind a legacy. They no longer had physical resources, but there was something else they had that could be passed on to those who would survive. So they chose to write down on paper the beliefs they held most dear and the values they most cherished. They called these documents ethical wills and put them in a vault at the synagogue. Here was their legacy to subsequent generations.

I have often thought how instructive this process could be for us today. If you knew that you were going to die tomorrow or face some terrible tragedy, and you needed to write to your children or grandchildren, passing on to them the best that was in your heart and mind, what would you say? Could you pick out the core values that define who you really are? What would they be? Are those values ones that others see in you—your spouse, your kids, your friends, the people at work? It is great to claim a set of values, but if you are not reflecting them in such a way that others can see them, are they really the values that are driving your life? Does your job define who you are, your salary, your title, your bank account, your home in the suburbs, your powerful position in the newspaper business or in a global business? Is it your car or your boat or your condo at the beach or in the mountains? Or is it your family, your caring, your willingness to reach out and serve others?

These are important questions for Americans to ask ourselves, for this nation was founded on a set of ethical standards and personal values that for most of the two hundred years since our founding have been the envy of the world. But it is no secret that our grasp of these values has been severely shaken in recent years. The reasons are complex, but certainly central among them are the frequency of people's moves, the propensity for materialism, the lust for power, and especially the collapse of the family as an institution.

The collapse of the family merits a closer look. Do you realize that today in the United States 50 percent of all marriages end in divorce, 22 percent of all babies are born out of wedlock, and 33 percent of all children will live with step-parents before they reach age 18? In our inner cities the situation is far worse. There, one finds no role models, no hope, and no incentive to improve or to escape. It is now common for welfare to extend across three generations in the same family. Babies are having babies. And often there are no fathers anywhere in sight. So, for many in the inner city the only hope is not a family life, because it does not exist; the only hope is the help that can come as business, social service agencies, and schools reach out to provide stability and values.

Regarding the formation of values, I don't believe they can be forced upon people. I do believe that we can talk about them, we can debate them, we can cause young people to focus on them so that they begin to mold the set of ethical standards and personal values that will help them. This is an on-going process. We go through it in elementary school, high school and college. We go through it at various thresholds in our lives—New Year's resolutions, the 30th birthday, the 40th, the 50th, etc. We are always redefining our values and priorities. We quickly learn that we face hard choices, for we cannot be all things to all people. Nor can we afford to drift through life without knowing who we are, without choosing the values that define us, and without reflecting those values in everything we do.

A clear statement of personal values is very important for each of us as persons, but, so too is it important for the businesses we lead. Later I shall say more about the importance of defining company values together with the people in your organization, but now I want to stress that if you are not clear about who you are as a person, you will not be able to be clear about what your company ought to be. Nor will your employees understand the values on which the company stands as it operates in the marketplace.

I now would like to say something about ten values that I think are particularly important in today's world. They are mentioned in no particular order. I hope they will cause you to think about what would constitute your own ethical will.

Ten important values

1. *Nurturing diversity.* We talk a lot about this but I am troubled today by the fact that there is more bigotry and hatred in our country than I have seen in a long time. We absolutely must get along within the heterogeneous population in our own country if we are ever going to get along with populations around the world.

By the year 2000, the United States will be a land dominated by minorities. I have had a first hand glimpse of this phenomenon, because I have lived in Miami for the past thirteen years where our population is 50 percent Hispanic, 30 percent Anglo, and 20 percent Black. In the past decade the total U.S. population grew by 12 percent, but the number of Asians increased by 127 percent and the number of Hispanics jumped by 59 percent. Today, four major cities already have lost their non-Latin, white majorities: Los Angeles, New York, San Antonio, and Miami. With this trend comes a complex mix of languages, cultures and values. This fact requires a process of constantly educating those who come freshly to our country as well as those who grow up in our country, so that we all understand and affirm the great values upon which our country was founded.

2. *Being accountable.* The U.S. Senate Chaplain, Dick Halberson, puts this problem well: "Too many of us demand freedom without restraint, rights without responsibility, choice without consequences, leisure without pain." I agree completely. I call it accountability. Too many have forgotten what it is. Michael Milken forgot it, Ivan Boesky forgot it, Reverend Jim Bakker forgot it, and so did Magic Johnson. I respect Magic Johnson's courage to reveal his battle with the HIV virus. But there is much more at stake than his message about safe sex. In his past relations with women, where was the notion of respect for others? Where was the notion of a caring, long-term relationship nurtured in a strong and respectful marriage? We read everyday about tragedies related to AIDS, date rape, drug addiction, child abuse, and sexual harassment. It all gets down to the question of whether we are going to respect the dignity of human life and be accountable for the way we relate to each other.

3. *Giving thanks.* I am constantly stunned at how few people simply take the time to thank someone for doing something important, whether it be at home with our family, or in our community, or in the workplace. I think this is especially important in times of stress, but in all times we need to do a much better job of thanking others for things they do for us.

4. *Being an encourager.* Each day there are dozens of people who cross our paths and need our encouragement. I suspect this happens more today than earlier, for with layoffs, drugs and the problems of crumbling family life, people are living under enormous stress. In these times a simple pat on the back can be very important. Author William Barclay makes my point very well: "It is easy to laugh at a person's ideals. It is easy to pour cold water on someone's enthusiasm. It is easy to discourage others. The world is full of discouragers. We have a duty to encourage one another."

5. *Nurturing a positive attitude toward life.* The business world is full of complainers and pessimists who think we can't get the

job done and believe that the company or the economy is going to hell. My guess is that our economy is better off than we might think and that some fundamental changes now occurring have been building in a positive direction for years. To have a positive attitude is very important. Charles Swindal says it well: "The longer I live, the more I realize the impact of attitude on life. It is more important than the past, than education, than money, than circumstances. It will make or break a company, a church, a home. I am convinced that life is ten percent what happens to me and ninety percent how I react to it."

6. *Building momentum.* None of us can get things done alone in our community, in our home, or in our business. We need to set a series of goals, to develop support for them, to get momentum going, to build on it, and to exude enthusiasm. If we stand around complaining and put off dealing with our problems, we shall never get the momentum going that needs to be a part of everything we do.

7. *Fostering trust.* I think the value of trust is ultimate in any personal or business relationship, whether at home or abroad. Trust is especially complex when you are dealing with other cultures and other languages, but it can never be taken for granted in anything we do. It gets to be a very personal issue in an individual's life. Trust starts in marriage, trust starts at work, trust starts with customers, trust starts with friends, it is in public life, it is in the way we do business with our colleagues and our partners abroad, it is everywhere we live.

And yet look at what has happened in American society. We install burglar alarms, we carry guns, we sign pre-nuptial agreements, we negotiate employment contracts, and we ask for payments in advance simply because no one trusts anybody today. Is it is not a chilling fact that in the United States 135,000 high school students carry guns to school each day? About one-quarter of the top, big-city high schools must put their students through metal detector devices, like those in airports, because the problem of guns in the halls and classrooms is so prevalent. What has happened to trust in America?

This is not an abstract goal remote from real life. Its presence or absence impacts everything we do, whether in our relationships with spouses and children, or at school, or in the workplace, or in doing business around the world. If we can't trust our spouse, our children, our candidate for President, our boss or our preacher, what is left that can hold our families and our society together?

8. *Supporting the family.* I have already spoken about this issue. Today, with the basic family unit crumbling, we need to turn more and more to what is called the extended family. Fortunately, many businesses today are addressing this need by adopting schools and encouraging their executives to be mentors, to be encouragers of fundamental values among young people who will never get those values at home because there is no home. The way by which we substitute for the crumbling traditional family with other vehicles in order to build fundamental values among youth is an extremely important issue for our nation's future.

9. *Preserving our religious underpinnings.* This nation was founded on Judeo-Christian values, but I believe we have gone so far to protect secularists' rights that we have given up our right and responsibility to articulate those religious underpinnings for our own time. I have worked very hard in my public life to respect the rights of others who believe differently from myself or don't believe at all. But I believe that those people have a responsibility to respect my religious values and to allow me the opportunity to speak out on the values that are ultimately important to me.

I think that those of us for whom religious faith is important need to be more effective in talking about the values that drove the first European settlers to come to this land, that moved later generations to formulate our Constitution and Bill of Rights, and that continue to guide many people in our nation today. I have no hesitancy in saying that my religious faith defines my values, it sets my moral compass, and it is absolutely essential to my own ethical will.

10. *Fostering volunteerism.* Volunteerism is a uniquely American tradition. Living in Miami has helped me appreciate this fact, because half of our population is from Latin America, where if the government doesn't undertake something for disadvantaged people, nobody will. The concept of giving your time and your financial resources for others has thrived in the United States, and I am pleased to note that it apparently is beginning now to take root in other parts of the world.

But today the need to help the disadvantaged of this nation has taken on fresh urgency, for we cannot expect the federal government, state governments or local governments to do it. Most of those entities are in deep financial trouble. As a result, citizens like us will have to step forward. There is a tremendous resource of care and compassion that can be tapped, and it is absolutely important that we continue to do that into the future.

The Knight-Ridder experience

So, I urge you to write down the values that make you the person you are, then share them with those you care the most about in life. I also urge you to go through the same process in your business. We did this at Knight-Ridder, and we call the resulting document the Knight-Ridder Promise. To formulate it, we had about twenty-five of our top executives spend two days together on three different occasions. They simply wrote one piece of paper, which I suspect was one of the most expensive pieces of paper in Knight-Ridder's history! But the fact of the matter is that we were developing ownership, and under the leadership of our Chairman and CEO, we put a lot of time into defining the ultimate values and basic goals that declared who we are as an institution. Then we have shared these with every one of our employees.

This is not a complicated, hard-to-understand document. In it we talk about Knight-Ridder as one of the world's leading publishing and information companies. We affirm that our enterprise is both a business and a public trust built on the highest standards of ethics and integrity. Our moral obligation is to excel in all that we do. Recognizing that change is inevitable, we welcome it and intend to benefit from it. Then we focus on our responsibilities to our customers, our employees, our shareholders, our communities and our society.

Every business needs to be clear—through this process or some other one—about what it stands for. We need to relate our values to everyday situations, and we who are leaders need to set a personal example in all that we do. To me there is nothing phonier than seeing someone who is a business leader espouse a set of values on paper but then fail to live them out in his actual deeds. I think also that it is important to recognize that our employees must understand what we expect of them and by what standards of measurement their performance will be evaluated.

I have been helped in my effort to concentrate on fundamental values by Robert Fulghrum's book, *All I Ever Really Needed to Know, I Learned in Kindergarten.* He has a lot of very practical advice for us. One of his concluding statements deserves citing: "Share everything, play fair, don't hit people, put things back where you found them, clean up your own mess, say you are sorry when you have hurt somebody, and when you go out into the world, watch out for traffic, hold hands and stick together." Not bad counsel for beginning our effort to define who we are and what we shall be in the future!

Part II

Academic Perspectives

6

Does Business Ethics Make Economic Sense?

Amartya Sen

1. Introduction

I begin not with the need for business ethics, but at the other end—the idea many people have that there is no need for such ethics. That conviction is quite widespread among practitioners of economics, though it is more often taken for granted implicitly rather than asserted explicitly. We must understand better what the conviction rests on and why it may be mistaken.

How did this idea of the redundancy of ethics get launched in economics? The early authors on economic matters, from Aristotle and Kautilya (in ancient Greece and ancient India respectively— the two were contemporaries, as it happens) to medieval practitioners (including Aquinas, Ockham, Maimonides, and others), to the economists of the early modern age (William Petty, Gregory King, François Quesnay, and others) were all much concerned, in varying degrees, with ethical analysis. In one way or another, they saw economics as a branch of "practical reason," in which concepts of the good, the right and the obligatory were quite central.

What happened then? As the "official" story goes, all this changed with Adam Smith, who can certainly be described as the father of modern economics. He made, so it is said, economics scientific and hard-headed, and the new economics that emerged in the nineteenth and twentieth centuries was all ready to do business, with no ethics to keep it tied to "morals and moralizing." That view of what happened is not only reflected in volumes of professional economics writings, but has even reached the status of getting into

P.M. Minus (ed.), *The Ethics of Business in a Global Economy.*

the English literature via a limerick by Stephen Leacock, who was both a literary writer and an economist:

> Adam, Adam, Adam Smith
> Listen what I charge you with!
> Didn't you say
> In a class one day
> That selfishness was bound to pay?
> Of all doctrines that was the Pith.
> Wasn't it, wasn't it, wasn't it, Smith?[1]

The interest in going over this bit of history (or alleged history) does not lie in scholastic curiosity. I believe it is important to see how that ethics-less view of economics and business emerged in order to understand what it is that is being missed. As it happens, that bit of potted history of "who killed business ethics" is altogether wrong, and it is particularly instructive to understand how the erroneous identification has come about.

2. Exchange, production and distribution

I go back, then, to Adam Smith. Indeed, he did try to make economics scientific, and to a great extent he was successful in this task, within the limits of what was possible then. While that part of the alleged history is right, what is altogether mistaken is the idea that Smith demonstrated, or believed he had demonstrated, the redundancy of ethics in economic and business affairs. Indeed, quite the contrary. The Professor of Moral Philosophy at the University of Glasgow—for that was Smith's position—was as interested in the importance of ethics in behavior as anyone could have been. It is instructive to see how the odd reading of Smith as a "no-nonsense" skeptic of economic and business ethics has come about.

Perhaps the most widely quoted remark of Adam Smith is the one about the butcher, the brewer and the baker in *The Wealth of Nations*: "It is not from the benevolence of the butcher, the brewer, or the baker that we expect our dinner, but from their regard to their own interest. We address ourselves, not to their humanity but to their self-love..."[2] The butcher, the brewer and the baker want our money, we want their products, and the exchange benefits us all.

There would seem to be no need for any ethics—business or otherwise—in bringing about this betterment of all the parties involved. All that is needed is regard for our own respective interests, and the market is meant to do the rest in bringing about the mutually gainful exchanges.

In modern economics this Smithian tribute to self-interest is cited again and again, indeed with such exclusivity that one is inclined to wonder whether this is the only passage of Smith that is read these days. What did Smith really suggest? Smith did argue in this passage that the pursuit of self-interest would motivate the exchange of commodities. But that is a very limited claim, even though it is full of wonderful insights in explaining why it is that we seek exchange and how exchange can be such a beneficial thing for all. But to understand the limits of what is being claimed here, we have to ask, first: Did Smith think that economic operations and business activities consist only of exchanges of this kind? Second, even in the context of exchange, we have to question: Did Smith think that the result would be just as good if the businesses involved, driven by self-interest, were to try to defraud the consumers, or the consumers in question were to attempt to swindle the sellers?

The answers to both these questions are clearly in the negative. The butcher-brewer-baker simplicity does not carry over to problems of production and distribution (and Smith never said that it did), nor to the problem of how a system of exchange can flourish institutionally. This is exactly where we begin to see why Smith could have been right in his claim about *the motivation for exchange* without establishing or trying to establish *the redundancy of business ethics* in general (or even in exchange).

The importance of self-interest pursuit is a helpful part of understanding many practical problems, for example, the supply problems in the former Soviet Union and Eastern Europe. But it is quite unhelpful in explaining the success of, say, Japanese economic performance vis-à-vis Western Europe or North America (since behavior modes in Japan are often deeply influenced by other conventions and pressures). Elsewhere in *The Wealth of Nations*, Adam Smith considers other problems which call for a more complex motivational structure. And in his *The Theory of Moral Sentiments*, Smith goes extensively into the need to go beyond profit maximization, arguing that "humanity, justice, generosity, and public spirit, are the qualities most useful to others."[3]

Adam Smith was very far from trying to deny the importance of ethics for behavior in general and for business behavior in particular.[4]

Through overlooking everything else that Smith said in his wide-ranging writings and concentrating only on this one butcher-brewer-baker passage, the father of modern economics is too often made to look like an ideologue. He is transformed into a partisan exponent of an ethics-free view of life which would have horrified Smith. To adapt a Shakespearian aphorism, while some men are born small and some achieve smallness, the unfortunate Adam Smith has had much smallness thrust upon him.

It is important to see how Smith's wholesome tribute to self-interest as a motivation for exchange (best illustrated in the butcher-brewer-baker passage) can co-exist peacefully with Smith's advocacy of ethical behavior elsewhere. Smith's concern with ethics was, of course, extremely extensive and by no means confined to economic and business matters. But since this is not the occasion to review Smith's ethical beliefs, but only to get insights from his combination of economic and ethical expertise to understand better the exact role of business ethics, we have to point our inquiries in that particular direction.

The butcher-brewer-baker discussion is all about *motivation for exchange*, but Smith was deeply concerned also with *production* as well as *distribution*. And to understand how exchange might itself actually work in practice, it is not adequate to concentrate only on the motivation that makes people *seek* exchange. It is necessary to look at the behavior patterns that could sustain a flourishing system of mutually profitable exchanges. The positive role of intelligent self-seeking in motivating exchange has to be supplemented by the motivational demands of production and distribution, and the systemic demands on the organization of the economy.

These issues are taken up now, linking the general discussion with practical problems faced in the contemporary world. In the next three sections I discuss in turn (1) the problem of organization (especially that of exchange), (2) the arrangement and performance of production, and (3) the challenge of distribution.

3. Organization and exchange: rules and trust

I come back to the butcher-brewer-baker example. The concern of the different parties with their own interests certainly can adequately *motivate* all of them to take part in the exchange from which each benefits. But whether the exchange would operate well would depend also on organizational conditions. This requires institutional development which can take quite some time to work—a lesson that is currently being learned rather painfully in Eastern Europe and the former Soviet Union. That point is now widely recognized, even though it was comprehensively ignored in the first flush of enthusiasm in seeking the magic of allegedly automatic market processes.

But what must also be considered now is the extent to which the economic institutions operate on the basis of common behavior patterns, shared trusts, and a mutual confidence in the ethics of the different parties. When Adam Smith pointed to the motivational importance of "regard to their own interest," he did not suggest that this motivation is all that is needed to have a flourishing system of exchange. If the baker cannot trust the householder, he may have difficulty in proceeding to produce bread to meet orders, or in delivering bread without prepayment. And the householder may not be certain whether he would be sensible in relying on the delivery of the ordered bread if the baker is not always altogether reliable. These problems of mutual confidence—discussed in a very simple form here—can be incomparably more complex and more critical in extended and multifarious business arrangements.

Mutual confidence in certain rules of behavior is typically implicit rather than explicit—indeed so implicit that its importance can be easily overlooked in situations where such confidence is widely shared. But in the context of (1) economic development across the Third World, and also of (2) institutional reform now sweeping across what used to be the Second World, these issues of behavioral norms and ethics can be altogether central.

In the Third World there is often also a deep-rooted skepticism about the reliability and moral quality of business behavior. This can be directed both at local businessmen and the commercial people from abroad. Such skepticism may sometimes be particularly galling to well established business firms including well-known multinationals. But the record of some powerful multinationals in dealing with the more vulnerable countries has left grounds for much suspicion, even though it may be misplaced in many cases. Establishing high standards of business ethics is certainly one way of tackling this problem.

In many Third World countries, there is also a traditional lack of confidence in the moral behavior of particular groups of traders, for example merchants of food grains. This is a subject on which—in the context of the-then Europe—Adam Smith himself commented substantially in *The Wealth of Nations*, though he thought these suspicions were by and large unjustified. In fact, the empirical record on this issue is quite diverse, and particular experiences of grain trade in conditions of scarcity and famine have left many questions to be answered.

This is an issue of extreme seriousness, since it is now becoming increasingly clear that typically the best way of organizing famine prevention and relief is to create additional incomes for the destitute (possibly through employment schemes) and then to rely on normal trade to meet the resulting food demand (through standard arrangements of transport and sales).[5] The alternative of bureaucratic distribution of food in hastily organized relief camps is often much slower, more wasteful, seriously disruptive of family life and normal economic operations, and more conducive to the spread of epidemic diseases. However, giving a crucial role to the grain traders at times of famine threats (as a complement to state-organized employment schemes to generate income) raises difficult issues of trust and trustworthiness: Can it be assumed that the traders will not manipulate the precarious situation in search of unusual profit? The issue of business ethics, thus, becomes an altogether vital part of the arrangement of famine prevention and relief.

The problem can be, to some extent, dealt with by skillful use of the threat of government intervention in the market. But the credibility of that threat depends greatly on the size of grain reserves the government itself has. It can work well in some cases (generally it has in India), but not others. Ultimately, much depends on the extent to which the relevant business people can establish exacting standards of behavior, rather than fly off in search of unusual profits to be rapidly extracted from manipulated situations.

I have been discussing problems of organization in exchange, and it would seem to be right to conclude this particular discussion by noting that the need for business ethics is quite strong even in the field of exchange (despite the near-universal presence of the butcher-brewer-baker motivations of "regard to their own interest"). If we now move on from exchange to production and distribution, the need for business ethics becomes even more forceful and perspicuous. The issue of trust is central to all economic operations. But we now have to consider other problems of interrelation in the process of production and distribution.

4. Organization of production: firms and public goods

Capitalism has been successful enough in generating output and raising productivity. But the experiences of different countries are quite diverse. The recent experiences of East Asian economies—most notably Japan—raise deep questions about the modeling of capitalism in traditional economic theory. Japan is often seen (rightly in a particular sense) as a great example of successful capitalism, but it is clear that the motivation patterns that dominate Japanese business have much more content than would be provided by pure profit maximization.

Different commentators have emphasized distinct aspects of Japanese motivational features. Michio Morishima has outlined the special characteristics of "Japanese ethos" as emerging from its particular history of rule-based behavior patterns.[6] Ronald Dore has seen the influence of "Confucian ethics."[7] Recently, Eiko Ikegami has pointed to the importance of the traditional concern with "honor"—a kind of generalization of the Samurai code—as a crucial modifier of business and economic motivation.[8]

Indeed, there is some truth, oddly enough, even in the puzzlingly witty claim made by *The Wall Street Journal* that Japan is "the only communist nation that works" (30 January 1989, p. 1). It is, as one would expect, mainly a remark about the non-profit motivations underlying many economic and business activities in Japan. We have to understand and interpret the peculiar fact that the most successful capitalist nation in the world flourishes economically with a motivation structure that departs firmly and often explicitly from the pursuit of self-interest, which is said to be the bedrock of capitalism.

In fact, Japan does not, by any means, provide the only example of a powerful role of business ethics in promoting capitalist success. The productive merits of selfless work and devotion to enterprise have been given much credit for economic achievements in many countries. Indeed, the need of capitalism for a motivational structure more complex than pure profit maximization has been acknowledged in various forms, over a long time, by various social scientists (though typically not by many "mainstream" economists): I have in mind Marx, Weber, Tawney, and others.[9] The basic point about the observed success of non-profit motives is neither unusual nor new, even though that wealth of historical and conceptual insights is often thoroughly ignored in professional economics today.

It is useful to bring this discussion in line with Adam Smith's concerns, and also with the general analytical approaches successfully developed in modern microeconomic theory. In order to understand how motives other than self-seeking can have an important role, we have to see the limited reach of the butcher-brewer-baker argument in dealing with what modern economists call "public goods." This becomes particularly relevant because the overall success of a modern enterprise is, in a very real sense, a public good.

But what *is* a public good? That idea can be best understood by contrasting it with a "private good," such as a toothbrush or a bicycle or an apple, which either you can use or I, but not both of us. Our respective uses would compete and be exclusive. This is not so with public goods, such as a livable environment or the absence of epidemics. All of us may benefit from breathing fresh air, living in an epidemic-free environment, and so on. When uses of commodities are non-competitive, as in the case of public goods, the rationale of the self-interest-based market mechanism comes under severe strain. The market system works by putting a price on a commodity and the allocation between consumers is done by the intensities of the respective willingness to buy it at the prevailing price. When "equilibrium prices" emerge, they balance demand with supply for each commodity. In contrast, in the case of public goods, the uses are—largely or entirely—non-competitive, and the system of giving a good to the highest bidder does not have much merit, since one person's consumption does not exclude that of another. Instead, optimum resource allocation would require that the *combined* benefits be compared with the costs of production, and here the market mechanism, based on profit maximization, functions badly.[10]

A related problem concerns the allocation of private goods involving strong "externalities," with interpersonal interdependencies working outside the markets. If the smoke from a factory makes a neighbor's home dirty and unpleasant, without the neighbor being able to charge the factory owner for the loss she suffers, then that is an "external" relation. The market does not help in this case, since it is not there to allocate the effects—good or bad—that work outside the market.[11] Public goods and externalities are related phenomena, and they are both quite common in such fields as public health care, basic education, environmental protection, and so on.

There are two important issues to address in this context, in analyzing the organization and performance of production. First, there tends to be some failure in resource allocation when the commodities produced are public goods or involve strong externalities. This recognition can be taken *either* (1) as an argument for having *publicly owned enterprises*, which would be governed by principles other than profit maximization, *or* (2) as a case for *public regulations* governing private enterprise, *or* (3) as establishing a need for the use of non-profit values—particularly of *social concern*—in private decisions (perhaps because of the goodwill that it might generate). Since public enterprises have not exactly covered themselves with glory in recent years, and public regulations, while useful, are sometimes quite hard to implement, the third option has become more important in public discussions. It is difficult to escape the argument for encouraging business ethics to go well beyond the traditional values of honesty and reliability, and to take on social responsibility as well (for example, in matters of environmental degradation and pollution).

The second issue is more complex and less recognized in the literature, but it is, in some ways, also more interesting. Even in the production of private commodities, there can be an important "public good" aspect in the production process itself. This is because production is a joint activity, supervisions are costly and often unfeasible, and each participant contributes to the overall success of the firm in a way that cannot be fully reflected in the private rewards that he or she gets.

The overall success of the firm, thus, is really a public good, from which all benefit, to which all contribute, and which is not parcelled out in little boxes of person-specific rewards strictly linked with each person's respective contribution. And this is precisely where motives other than narrow self-seeking become productively important. Even though I do not have the opportunity to pursue the point further here, I do believe that the successes of "Japanese ethos," "Confucian ethics," "Samurai codes of honor," etc., can be fruitfully linked to this aspect of the organization of production.

5. The challenge of distribution: values and incentives

I turn now to distribution. It is not hard to see that non-self-seeking motivations can be extremely important for *distributional* problems in general. In dividing a cake, one person's gain is another's loss. At a very obvious level, the contributions that can be made by ethics—business ethics and others—include the amelioration of misery through policies explicitly aimed at such a result. There is an extensive literature on donations, charity, and philanthropy in general, and also on the willingness to join in communal activities geared to social improvement. The connection with ethics is obvious enough in these cases.

What is perhaps more interesting to discuss is the fact that distributional and productional problems very often come mixed together, so that how the cake is divided influences the size of the cake itself. The so-called "incentive problem" is a part of this relationship. This too is a much discussed problem,[12] but it is important to clarify in the present context that the extent of the conflict between size and distribution depends crucially on the motivational and behavioral assumptions. The incentive problem is not an immutable feature of production technology. For example, the more narrowly profit-oriented an enterprise is, the more it would, in general, tend to resist looking after the interests of others—workers, associates, consumers. This an area in which ethics can make a big difference.

The relevance of all this to the question we have been asked to address ("Does business ethics make economic sense?") does, of course, depend on how "economic sense" is defined. If economic sense includes the achievement of a good society in which one lives, then the distributional improvements can be counted in as parts of sensible outcomes even for business. Visionary industrialists and businessmen have tended to encourage this line of reasoning.

On the other hand, if "economic sense" is interpreted to mean nothing other than achievement of profits and business rewards, then the concerns for others and for distributional equity have to be judged entirely instrumentally, in terms of how they indirectly help to promote profits. That connection is not to be scoffed at, since firms that treat their workers well are often very richly rewarded for it. For one thing, the workers are then more reluctant to lose their jobs, since more would be sacrificed if dismissed from this (more lucrative) employment, compared with alternative opportunities. The contribution of goodwill to team spirit and thus to productivity can also be quite plentiful.

We have then an important contrast between two different ways in which good business behavior could make economic sense. One way is to see the improvement of the society in which one lives as a reward in itself; this works directly. The other is to use ultimately a business criterion for evaluation, taking note of the extent to which good business behavior could lead to favorable business performance; this enlightened self-interest involves an indirect reasoning.

It is often hard to disentangle the two features, but in understanding whether or how business ethics makes economic sense, we have to take note of each feature. If, for example, a business firm pays inadequate attention to the safety of its workers, and this results accidentally in a disastrous tragedy, like the one that happened in Bhopal some years ago (though I am not commenting at present on the extent to which Union Carbide was in fact negligent there), that event would be harmful both for the firm's profits and for the general objectives of social well-being in which the firm may be expected to take an interest. The two effects are distinct and separable, but business ethics has to relate to both.

6. A concluding remark

I end with a brief recapitulation of some of the points discussed. First, the importance of business ethics is not contradicted in any way by Adam Smith's pointer to the fact that our "regards to our own interest" provide adequate motivation for exchange (section 2). Smith's butcher-brewer-baker argument is concerned (1) directly with *exchange* only (not production or distribution), and (2) only with the *motivational aspect* of exchange (not its organizational and behavioral aspects).

Second, business ethics can be crucially important in economic organization in general and in exchange operations in particular. This relationship is extensive and fairly ubiquitous, but it is particularly important at this time for the development efforts of the Third World and the reorganizational attempts in what formerly was the Second World (section 3).

Third, the importance of business ethics in the arrangement and performance of production can be illustrated by the contrasting experiences of different economies, for example by Japan's unusual success. The advantages of going beyond the pure pursuit of profit can be understood in different ways. To some extent, this question relates to the failure of profit-based market allocation in dealing with "public goods." This is relevant in two different ways: (1) the presence of public goods (and of the related phenomenon of externalities) in the commodities produced (e.g., environmental connections), and (2) the fact that the success of the firm can itself be fruitfully seen as a public good (section 4).

Finally, distributional problems are particularly related to behavioral ethics. The connections can be direct and valuational, as well as indirect and instrumental. The interrelations between the size of the cake and its distribution increase the reach and relevance of ethical behavior, e.g., through the incentive problem (section 5).

References

1. Stephen Leacock, *Hellements of Hickonomics* (New York: Dodd, Mead & Co, 1936), p. 75.

2. Adam Smith, *An Inquiry into the Nature and Causes of the Wealth of Nations* (1776; republished, London: Dent, 1910), vol. I, p. 13.

3. Adam Smith, *The Theory of Moral Sentiments* (revised edition, 1790; reprinted, Oxford: Clarendon Press, 1976), p. 189.

4. On this and related matters, see my *On Ethics and Economics* (Oxford: Blackwell, 1987); Patricia H. Werhane, *Adam Smith and His Legacy for Modern Capitalism* (New York: Oxford University Press, 1991); Emma Rothschild, "Adam Smith and Conservative Economics," *Economic History Review*, 1992 (forthcoming).

5. On this see Jean Drèze and Amartya Sen, *Hunger and Public Action* (Oxford: Clarendon Press, 1989).

6. Michio Morishima, *Why Has Japan 'Succeeded'? Western Technology and Japanese Ethos* (Cambridge University Press, 1982).

7. Ronald Dore, "Goodwill and the Spirit of Market Capitalism," *British Journal of Sociology*, 34 (1983), and *Taking Japan Seriously: A Confucian Perspective on Leading Economic Issues* (Stanford: Stanford University Press, 1987).

8. Eiko Ikegami, "The Logic of Cultural Change: Honor, State-Making, and the Samurai," mimeographed, Department of Sociology, Yale University, 1991.

9. Karl Marx (with F. Engels), *The German Ideology* (1845-46, English translation, New York: International Publishers, 1947); Richard Henry Tawney, *Religion and the Rise of Capitalism* (London: Murray, 1926); Max Weber, *The Protestant Ethic and the Spirit of Capitalism* (London: Allen & Unwin, 1930).

10. The classic treatment of public goods and provided by Paul A. Samuelson, "The Pure Theory of Public Expenditure," *Review of Economics and Statistics*, 35 (1954).

11. For a classic treatment of external effects, see A.C. Pigou, *The Economics of Welfare* (London: Macmillan, 1920). There are many different ways of defining "externalities," with rather disparate bearings on policy issues; on this see the wide-ranging critical work of Andreas Papandreou (Jr., I should add to avoid any ambiguity, though I don't believe he uses that clarification), *Ideas of Externality*, to be published by Clarendon Press, Oxford, and Oxford University Press, New York.

12. A good general review of the literature can be found in A.B. Atkinson and J.E. Stiglitz, *Lectures on Public Economics* (New York: McGraw-Hill, 1980).

7

When in Rome, Do...What?
International Business and Cultural Relativism

Thomas Donaldson

Our moral intuitions frequently blur when we go to Rome—that is, when we cross the line of our nation's boundaries. Without the backdrop of approximate moral consensus that exists within a culture and without sets of laws and judicial procedures that define standards of minimal conduct, moral clarity is elusive. When, as U.S. or French managers, for example, we ask whether it is permissible to make new investments in nations where civil rights and political rights are violated, or to refuse to hire female managers in Saudi Arabia, our intuitions can fail us. When we ask whether it is permissible to circumvent restrictive environmental or occupational health laws at home by shifting facilities to poor developing nations, or to fill management and senior technical positions in a host nation with nationals from the home country, we are forced to abandon norms that are merely *nation-specific* and move to principles that transcend national boundaries.

But what are such principles, and what are their limits?

Facing moral problems in international business requires more than good intentions. Even the best-informed, best-intentioned executive must re-think intuitions in mixed cultural contexts. Even when those intuitions are fundamentally sound, they have been honed in relatively simple, home-culture contexts. The same intuitions that serve well in a homogeneous context can fail when home and host norms conflict. Hence even the traditional litmus test, "What would people think of your actions if they were written up on the front page of the newspaper?", is an unreliable guide. For in international contexts there exist strikingly different sets of newspaper readers.

As we step beyond the boundaries of our nation state, we enter a realm where domestic law is notoriously inefficient and where many nation states have difficulty efficiently regulating foreign transnational corporations. From time to time, unscrupulous companies have exploited this problem to their own advantage. As James Brooke noted in the *New York Times* (July 17, 1988), during 1988 virtually every country from Morocco to the Congo on Africa's west coast was approached by companies who wanted cheap sites for dumping waste. In February of that year, officials in Guinea Bissau, one of the world's poorest nations, agreed to bury fifteen million tons of toxic wastes from European tanneries and pharmaceutical companies. The companies agreed to pay about $120 million, which is only slightly less than the country's entire gross national product. Brooke also described how in Nigeria in 1987 five European ships unloaded toxic waste containing dangerous poisons such as polychlorinated biphenyls, or PCB's. Workers wearing thongs and shorts unloaded the barrels for $2.50 a day and placed them in a dirt lot in a residential area in the town of Kiko. They were not told about the contents of the barrels.

One may decry the political inefficiency that tolerated such a human and environmental tragedy, but the fact is that many Third World governments resemble Nigeria in being unable to police transnationals adequately.

Hence, neither a simple-minded extension of home morality, nor domestic law is the answer. But what is?

Relativism is not the answer

One answer to this question is as old as philosophical discussion, and as old as Sophistry. Its label is "cultural relativism," and it is a view that holds that no culture has a better ethics than any other, and that, in turn, there are no international "rights" and "wrongs." If Thailand tolerates the bribery of public officials, then Thai tolerance is no worse than Japanese or German intolerance. If Switzerland fails to find insider trading morally repugnant, then Swiss liberality is no worse than U.S. fair-mindedness. The concept of cultural relativism is fairly simple to grasp, and unfortunately, fairly tempting when business opportunities are at stake.

We should first note one of the most prevalent confusions about relativism and ethics, namely, that of equating cultural relativism with *tolerance*. What most of us have in mind when we shy away from absolute moral pronouncements is exactly the opposite of relativism. When we deny that one country should dictate its morality for another, and when we encourage respect for the different customs of foreign peoples, we are actually citing a universal, trans-cultural value. That is, if we believe that the United States ought not force its modern democratic method of government on Muslim countries, then we similarly believe that *all other countries* ought not impose democratic methods on Muslim countries. And, in turn, we expect *Muslim countries* not to impose their form of government on other, non-Muslim countries. Tolerance is a universalizable moral value; and it is a far cry from relativism.

In the final analysis, relativism must be rejected. Perhaps its main problem is that not all cultural differences lie at the fairly inconsequential level of insider trading or petty bribery. If one seriously maintains the view of cultural relativism, one must be prepared to tolerate *all* cultural differences. If one state endorses piracy (as some in history have), then one must grant piracy the same moral status as a doctrine of anti-piracy. Or consider the dramatic example of crime prevention in ancient Rome. There it was the practice to kill *all* of the slaves in a household in the event that one slave murdered the master. All slaves were lined up and summarily executed without trial. They were executed whether they were young or old, male or female, and whether or not they were involved in, or had any knowledge about, the murder. In some instances involving large households, the practice resulted in the execution of three and four hundred innocent persons. While the practice was justified on the grounds that it deterred future plots against the master, few of us today could embrace such reasoning. And in the light of heinous practices such as this, few of us can cling to theoretical relativism that would tolerate these or even worse practices. Hence, if we reject relativism in the extreme instances, then morality in the international sphere must be something more than an unprincipled, "do-what-the-natives-do" undertaking. It does not follow that *all* questions of moral differences among cultures can be solved by measuring them against a rigid, universal yardstick. But it means that morality has some, albeit imperfect, relevance to transcultural contexts.

Codes are not the answer

I interpret international codes of ethics as part of a much broader movement to formalize the principles of business conduct. No one can deny that corporate codes and other, formal, agreed-upon principles provide managers with a good first step in approaching moral issues. Let us delineate four distinct categories of attempts at what Lee Preston has called "international public policy." International attempts to formulate principles of business conduct may be divided into four general headings: inter-firm, inter-government, cooperative, and world-organizational efforts. The first category of "inter-firm" standards reflects initiatives from industries, firms, and consumer groups. It includes the numerous inter-industry codes of conduct that are operative for international business, such as the Sullivan Standards for fair business practice in South Africa, the World Health Organization's Code on Pharmaceuticals and Tobacco, and the World Intellectual Property Organization's Revision of the Paris Convention for the Protection of Industrial Patents and Trademarks. The second category of "inter-government" efforts includes specific-purpose arrangements between and among nation states, such as the General Agreement on Tariffs and Trade (GATT) the International Monetary Fund (IMF), and the World Bank. "Cooperative" efforts, which comprise the third category, involve governments and industries coordinating skills in mutual arrangements that regulate international commerce. The European Community (EC) and the Andean Common Market (ANCOM) are two notable examples of such cooperative efforts. Finally, the fourth or "world-organizational" category includes efforts from broadly based global institutions such as the World Court, the International Labor organization (ILO), the Organization for Economic Cooperation and Development (OECD), and the various sub-entities of the United Nations.[1]

But having said this, one should acknowledge serious problems with ethical codes in business when relied upon to ensure acceptable levels of international conduct. Codes are inexact instruments for handling exact problems. For example, IBM's renowned Business Conduct Guidelines are necessarily general and cannot be construed to cover the niceties of every problem. Nor can any code. Additionally, codes always speak in the language of "thou shalt nots." Surely it is not always true that as one's knowledge of the restrictive principles that are the "thou shalt nots," i.e., of the bare minimums, becomes more detailed, one becomes more ethical. One is not necessarily more ethical after getting a law degree.

Finally, codes are often the "fig leaf" used to cover past and present corporate sins. In the U. S., researchers have detected a slight *negative* correlation between a company's having a code of ethics and criminal misconduct. This is probably not because codes cause criminal misconduct, but because those companies with tendencies towards criminal misconduct will adopt codes to resolve the problem, or to raise their fallen public image. Yet the absence of a strong positive correlation between having a code and avoiding criminal misconduct highlights the fact that codes are no panacea.

Shaping an answer

A guiding dictum for framing an answer to the "When in Rome..." problem is to steer a middle course between moral absolutism on the one hand, which says, "Our culture is the best, and you had better conform," and relativism on the other, which says, "look, if they tolerate this in their culture, then it's their business." Somehow, we must be able to say to Union Carbide, "You goofed. You committed a tragic mistake in letting safety precautions lapse in Bhopal," while maintaining a certain degree of tolerance in regards to the non-Western cultural traditions of India.

In steering between these two rocks, there are a number of concepts which can be helpful, perhaps the most important of which I would call a "moral threshold" for corporate behavior abroad. There are many different languages which can be used to create this threshold, such that when a corporation falls beneath it, the corporation can be told, "You've made a moral mistake," even in contexts where host country practices allow the company's behavior. Probably the most popular language in the world for establishing such a threshold is the language of rights. And the U.N.'s Universal Declaration of Human Rights is only one example of the way in which countries have tried collectively to specify absolute minimums of moral conduct.

We can learn a great deal by framing a moral threshold in terms of rights, and by understanding the implications such rights have for corporate behavior. Moral philosophers tell us that whenever there is a right, there is not only a duty to avoid depriving people of the right directly, but also a duty to protect people from its deprivation. Companies encounter this kind of situation frequently. Surveys of people in Central America show that the average Central American went to work at the age of eleven. If we believe in the right to a minimum education, which includes, at the very least, the ability to read and write, then surely hiring very young children for ongoing full-time labor fails the moral threshold test. The corporation doing this has failed to protect the basic human right to a minimal education from deprivation. Or suppose a corporation is considering buying land in a Third World country owned by a few wealthy landowners. Imagine that for years the land was used by peasants working as sharecroppers, who returned a significant portion of the crop that they harvested to the owners and retained the rest of it for their own nutritional needs. Suppose also that the corporation is aware that by buying the land and converting it to produce a cash crop, such as coffee or flowers, it will force people to migrate to the city slums, which, in turn, will result in their suffering serious malnutrition. Despite the fact that, as Coleridge said, people would die so slowly that none dare call it "murder," the right to subsistence, championed in many international documents, would have been violated by the corporation's purchase and conversion of the land.

Utilizing the concept of a right is also helpful because rights establish bare minimums of ethical behavior without the ring of absolutism. We should reject the possibility of a system of principles that is excessively universal and which neglects the moral freedom of particular cultures, nations, industries and corporations.

Limits to universal principles

The rejection of cultural relativism and the adoption of universal principles, such as those establishing a minimal floor for corporate behavior, must respect cultural and economic differences. Even if general values were exactly the same around the world, the same specific principles would not necessarily be appropriate for every host country context. For example, virtually everyone shares the values of pollution abatement and economic development, yet tradeoffs may be rationally made in a different direction by a struggling, Third World country on the one hand, and a highly developed one on the other. At a level of economic development where people remain malnourished or starving, a country may rationally adopt a different principle for regulating water pollution than were it at a higher level. For example, it may adopt a slightly lower standard of thermal water pollution than that observed in the U.S. or Japan (resulting in more lower fish species, such as carp, and fewer higher fish species, such as trout). Once it reaches the higher level of development it too will opt for more trout. But for the time-being it would prefer fertilizer.

Furthermore, a communitarian basis is required by any living doctrine of ethics. In this regard the ethics of international business is no different from the ethics of family or neighborhood; indeed business ethics is perhaps even more communitarian than traditional morality because of the amazingly plastic institutions it must encompass. As I have argued recently in a paper with Thomas Dunfee, correct ethical behavior in business contexts must be defined not only in relation to abstract and universal normative ideals, but also in relation to the moral understandings of living members of economic systems and organizations.[2] An important source of normative standards for international business behavior must be the set of implicit agreements which constitute the psychological reality of everyday economic life. We must, in other words, combine universally applicable norms of fairness and respect for persons with the range of what may be called "extant social contracts," i.e., with the specificity of moral agreements within and among industries, firms, departments, professions, and business cultures.

To understand this point better, imagine for a moment that you are a master of moral theory. You have read and absorbed the moral theories from Aristotle's eudaemonism and Chinese Confucianism to Kant's categorical imperative and Sidgewick's methods of ethics. Imagine further that you have either determined which one of these traditional theories is best or have constructed a wholly new "best" theory using parts of existing theories. Now imagine that someone asks you to define "unethical insider trading." Will you be able to provide a satisfactory answer without faking it? Will you be able to know the correct course of action in all cultures where insider trading is at issue?

So long as the only thing you knew were "the best moral theory," you would be hard-pressed to produce a satisfactory definition of unethical insider trading, or to know the correct course of action in all cultures. This is because moral rationality is what may be called "bounded," and it is especially so in cross-cultural, economic contexts.

By "bounded" I mean that otherwise rational moral agents when applying moral theory to actual situations confront at least two kinds of limit. First, they must acknowledge their own finite ability to apprehend and absorb the complexity and detail relevant to any ethical context. Each potential action has infinite consequences, and many of these are relevant to a moral evaluation of the act. But a finite mind cannot comprehend an infinite array of consequences. This aspect of the "boundedness" of moral rationality is similar to Herbert Simon's concept of "boundedness." Human beings have finite intellectual capacity and will inevitably "satisfice," that is, they will make decisions that fall short of what perfect rationality requires.

Second, moral decision-making in foreign business cultures is hampered by the highly "artifactual" nature of economic systems and practices. Economic systems and practices are "artifacts," which is to say that we *make* them what they are, and we can—and often do—choose to make them differently. The rules of the economic "game" vary enormously from culture to culture, and from company to company. For example, even among cultures championing the concept of private property, widely varying interpretations exist of what private property means. And just as the ethics of basketball must be contoured to the rules of basketball, so too the ethics of a given economic system must be contoured to the rules of that system.[3] The problem is not resolved simply by discovering and following whatever moral rules exist in a given economic system, for, as we have seen, ethics means more than cultural relativism.

For the topic of ethics in international business, the upshot of the boundedness of moral rationality is that no culture can claim to "see" with perfect vision the moral truth in economic affairs. Yet any culture, especially in its economic life, must reduce normative uncertainty in business as it structures its business relations in a way that is predictable and understandable. For this reason, we allow different cultures a certain amount of *latitude in defining for themselves their economic morality*.

This acknowledgment does not reduce to the relativistic view that any economic morality is as good as any other. Certainly there exist what Thomas Dunfee and I have chosen to call "hypernorms," or, in other words, norms so fundamental to the human condition that they have transcultural implications. One of the key hypernorms for assessing international business conduct is the notion of a fundamental right discussed earlier. Another would be the maintenance, through any action or policy, of the equal respect and dignity due every human person. Any economic culture that defined economic morality in a way that accorded unequal dignity to each human person, or that systematically violated human rights, could have no claim to legitimacy. Hence, Dunfee and I argue that hypernorms include at least the following:

—core human rights, including those to personal freedom, physical security and well-being, political participation, informed consent, and the ownership of property; and

—the obligation to accord equal dignity to each human person.[4]

To illustrate, we would expect that the hypernorm requiring recognition of the equal dignity of each person prohibits exclusion from fundamental economic and political activities based on race or gender.

Nonetheless, because of bounded rationality and the ensuing freedom of each culture to define within limits economic morality for itself, it is not true that all cultures must define insider trading, or impermissible gifts to business acquaintances, in precisely the same way.[5] And while the hypernorm requiring recognition of the equal dignity of each human probably requires that corporations extend help to customers accidentally harmed by its products, the amount of help morally required can vary from culture to culture. Consider the Japanese practice of having the CEO of an airline company visit the victims of an airline crash. In the United States, we possess a well-developed—some would say litigious—adversarial system for delivering compensation to victims. But in Japan and elsewhere the legal system for delivering compensation is less developed and less reliable. Hence, somewhat greater moral burdens are placed on Japanese corporate officials than on their U. S. counterparts. In short, a culture's traditional emphasis—or lack of emphasis—on the relevance of law to business, its conception of the role of the market in securing certain public goods, and its conception of the relationship between economic life and religious life, all can affect the determination of business morality.

Hence, it does not follow that simply because culture A's conception of insider trading is different from B's, one of the two is wrong. In short, we must eschew mono-moralism in economic affairs just as we eschew cultural relativism. When in Rome we should not simply do as the Romans, nor exactly as we do at home. We should allow for differences in customs even as we remain true to our own deeper values at home; and doing this well means preparing for our trip to Rome in advance.

References

1. For a more complete account of these various categories, see Thomas Donaldson, *The Ethics of International Business* (Oxford University Press, 1989), Chapter 3.

2. I have articulated this view more completely in "Integrative Social Contracts Theory: Ethics in Economic Life," an unpublished paper coauthored with Thomas Dunfee.

3. A third form of limit contributes to bounded moral rationality which for reasons of space I shall not describe in detail. Moral rationality is bounded by the limited ability of moral theory to model moral convictions and preferences. No matter how intricate the theory, it may miss key moral convictions that we rely upon and take for granted in ordinary life. While I will not discuss this concept of boundedness further, it has been examined recently by current philosophical writers such as Bernard Williams and Andrew Oldenquist.

4. There is substantial support for this initial list of hypernorms. For example, the proposed text of the draft United Nations Code of conduct of Transnational Corporations provides in paragraph 14 that "Transnational corporations shall respect human rights and fundamental freedoms in the countries in which they operate. In their social and industrial relations, transnational corporations shall not discriminate on the basis of race, color, sex, religion...." (United Nations, 1990)

5. When rules conflict between cultures, the question of which rule to use can arise. To arbitrate such disputes, Professor Dunfee and I have articulated a set of "priority principles" as follows:
   A. Transactions solely within a single community, which do not have significant adverse effects on other humans or communities, should be governed by the host community's norms.
   B. Community norms for resolving priority should be applied, so long as they do not have significant adverse effects on other humans or communities.

C.   The more extensive or more global the community which is the source of the norm, the greater the priority which should be given to the norm.

D.   Norms essential to the maintenance of the environment in which the transaction occurs should have priority over norms potentially damaging to that environment.

E.   Where multiple conflicting norms are involved, patterns of consistency among the alternative norms provides a basis for prioritization.

F.   Well-defined norms should ordinarily have priority over more general, less precise norms.

8

Developing Ethical Standards for International Business: What Roles for Business and Government?

Richard T. De George

How does a company with integrity[1] compete in international business? The short answer, from an ethical point of view, is: with care and with difficulty. The care needed involves gathering knowledge of and being sensitive to different customs, mores, ethical viewpoints, and cultural norms as the company moves from country to country. The difficulty stems from the lack of international enforcement of standards to keep competition fair, from the fact that governments are set up to foster the interests of the people they represent, and from the present-day reality that although business is global, there is no effective or efficient way of dealing with problems--such as the depletion of the ozone level--that fall beyond the competence of both individual corporations and individual governments.

Several myths compound the difficulty of the corporation with integrity. One is the Myth of Amoral International Business. The second is the Lack of Standards Myth. The third is the Myth of Government as Watchdog.

Given this situation and the prevalent myths, what can and what should a company with integrity do to compete successfully? Can a company with integrity compete ethically when its competitors do not abide by the same rules it follows and when self-policing puts it at a competitive disadvantage? The answer is yes. The issue is how to reduce the difficulty of so acting.

P.M. Minus (ed.), *The Ethics of Business in a Global Economy*.

The three myths

1.   The first myth is the Myth of Amoral International Business.[2] Like many myths, this one states a partial truth and hides a portion of reality that it cannot adequately handle. The myth claims that ethics, values and standards have no place in international business. It claims further that business on the international level in fact operates without such standards, and that anyone or any business that attempts to abide by standards puts itself foolishly at a competitive disadvantage. The myth does state what many people both in and out of business believe about international business. It also represents the attitude of some firms, which seek to maximize profits and pay as little attention to standards, rules, or laws as they can get away with.

The myth, however, ignores the fact that not all firms behave this way. It also ignores the fact that doing business on the international level, just as on the national level, presupposes certain basic standards without which business would be impossible. Unless the goods received are of the quality anticipated, there will be no renewed purchases. Unless payment is received for goods, there will be no transaction.   Unless one's agreements or contracts or understandings are honored in most industries most of the time, commerce grinds to a halt. Violations of these norms are necessarily the exception if business is to continue. Formulating the obvious into codes may serve some purpose, whether done by firms, industries, or governments.   But whether or not some company, industry, government or group codifies these norms is not essential. Rather, basic standards such as these exist because they are necessary in practice and are the bedrock on which business is built.

The myth also ignores and is unable to explain scandals and public protest against violations of basic norms. An event is a scandal only if perceived by the public as an act of wrongdoing. The Valdez incident, the Bhopal disaster, the BCCI debacle, the many insider trading and financial manipulation cases in the United States, Britain, and Japan,[3] the abuses of pension and other funds by Robert Maxwell on an international level,[4] and the many charges made against multinational drug companies are all evidence that people do not accept the Myth of Amoral International Business. If they did, each of these would simply be considered business as usual and would not provoke moral outrage and condemnation. The myth is unable to explain such moral reaction, because the myth claims morality has no role to play in business.

2. The second myth is the Lack of Standards Myth. Surprisingly perhaps, this myth permeates the thinking and work even of many of those engaged in business ethics. It says that there are no accepted international standards governing business, and that therefore any company of integrity must develop them from scratch. Businesses, academic consultants, and conferences are fond of discussing and proposing standards for international business as if none existed. The typical results are exercises in reinventing the wheel. The myth reflects a common perception of an absence of standards, the little attention often given to existing standards, and the lack of enforcement for most of them. But the myth covers over and ignores the many already existing standards. The standards available are of four sorts, and it is from these that any company with integrity, that any industry, that any conference or governmental or non-governmental body should start.

A) The first are the norms necessary in order to carry on business or trade of any kind, which I have already mentioned. Added to these are the common rules of morality that are so widely held as to be universal--such as recognition that arbitrary killing or torture of human beings is unethical--and the rights listed in such documents as the Universal Declaration of Human Rights,[5] which has been signed by most nations of the world and serves at least as a standard to which people can point and appeal.

B) Beyond these, people frequently ask: Whose standards shall we follow, as if standards are a grab-bag from which one can pick and chose at will. For a company of integrity the answer is one's own standards. A company of integrity has standards, values, principles or beliefs that it articulates and in accordance with which it acts. Its standards are not arbitrary, but are such that it is willing to announce them publicly, the assumption being that they are publicly defensible. In the United States a large percentage of the Fortune 500 firms have codes of conduct.[6] They vary considerably in what they cover and in the extent to which they specify ethical norms. Not all companies with a code act in accordance with them or are companies of integrity. But any company of integrity will implement its code wherever it operates. Since it is a public document, its shareholders, customers, and the general public can hold the company to its own code wherever the company operates. To assume that companies will act unethically whenever they can in order to maximize profits is to assume more than the facts show. But clearly a company with integrity will have to consider carefully how its code translates in the different national contexts in which it does business. It also does not set up its standards in a vacuum, and they must cohere with other existing recognized or agreed upon standards. Nonetheless its own standards give it a basis from which to discuss, consider, and negotiate other standards in the international arena.

C) Of central importance as standards to consider are those that have been hammered out since the late 1970s by the UN Commission on Transnational Corporations.[7] Although not all of these standards are ethical standards, many of them are, such as "respect for human rights and fundamental freedom" (item 14), "abstention from corrupt practices" (item 20), standards on transfer pricing (item 33), consumer protection (items 37-40), environmental protection (items 41-43), and the disclosure of information (item 44). Moreover, on most of them agreement has been reached. There are still a few unresolved issues, one being the provision that in effect adopts the standard of the American Foreign Corrupt Practices Act.[8]

Nations that accept these standards may either accept them as goals or adopt them into national legislation. But all the work that has gone into the Commission's document clearly should be a starting point for both national standards and a variety of more specific industry or business codes.

D) The fourth point of reference is the industry-wide codes that presently exist. Two types are most significant. One type is exemplified by the WHO Code governing the sale of infant formula, to which the infant formula companies worldwide have agreed.[9] In those countries where enforcement is not written into law, the public and certain groups have acted as watchdogs, monitoring compliance. Purported failure (denied by Nestlé) to live up to the code led, for instance, to the call by some critics for a renewal of the Nestlé boycott.[10]

The second type of code is exemplified by the industry-wide code of the chemical industry. Following Bhopal and other disasters, the chemical industry worldwide took the initiative in developing a code that attempts to guarantee the safety of chemical plants and to diminish any possible harm the plants might do. In 1988 the Chemical Manufacturers Association of the United States adopted a

"Responsible Care" program. Two years later over 170 member companies of the Chemical Manufacturers Association, in full page ads in the *New York Times* and the *Wall Street Journal*, announced the Guiding Principles to which they committed themselves.[11] Since 1990 the chemical manufacturers of various countries have adopted codes of practice based on the Guiding Principles, have adopted specific targets to improve their safety performance, and have set up norms against which they can be judged and they can judge themselves. There are no official sanctions for failure to comply, but companies committed to the principles indicate that they will apply peer pressure to help ensure compliance. This is industry self-regulation that perhaps was undertaken in order to preclude governmental regulation. Nonetheless, it is self-regulation worldwide, with the pressure for compliance coming from the other members of the industry itself. It serves as a model for other industries as well. Companies of integrity in each industry can take the lead in articulating appropriate industry norms and in committing themselves to living up to them.

3. The third myth is the Myth of Government As Watchdog. This is an American myth that presupposes a certain model of business and government and of their relation, which is neither dominant worldwide, nor even entirely appropriate in any country. The model is one where government and business are in an antagonistic relation, with government legislating certain restrictions on business that business would rather not have and that government might not impose if business regulated itself in such a way as to do no harm to the environment, its customers, or the general population. Pollution control within a given country is a typical example. The model is a myth not because government never sets standards and regulates business, but because important as it is, in international business this is only one part of a complex government-business relation. While a government may impose pollution controls on its industries at home, it may simultaneously fight against treaties or plans that impose more stringent pollution controls on its industries demanded or sought by other countries.

Rather than government as watchdog, a very close link exists between government and business in many parts of the world. Even in the United States, that link is symbolically typified by President Bush's bringing with him three auto industry executives when he went to negotiate trade agreements with Japan in January 1992. Clearly governments, especially in the international domain, protect their home industries. It is for this reason, for instance, that so many governments have resisted adopting laws comparable to the American Foreign Corrupt Practices Act. Governments' desire to protect business interests make many treaties difficult to conclude.

The internal function of government varies from government to government. In a socialist type government such as that found in the former USSR and in China today, government in effect is the owner and operator of business. The interests of business are the interests of government, since the government is both the owner of resources and factories, the employer of the workers, and the regulator of both prices and wages. To the extent that the government precludes the direct exploitation of one individual by another through hiring, it protects its citizens. By excluding competition, it does not have the problems of keeping competition fair. But since such a government regulates industry, and so regulates itself, it has no checks on its regulation. In the case of the Soviet Union and the countries of Eastern and Central Europe, this led to great abuses and to great environmental degradation. In countries with corrupt governments, government often acts in concert with business to the detriment of the country and its non-elite population.

In countries with mixed economies the role of government in the publicly-owned industries is one of employer and owner, and in the private sector one of arbitrator and regulator. How much the government regulates business varies from country to country. In a country like Japan, which is not socialist but in which an important function of government is to support and protect especially its large industries, the element of control is clearly less than in the American scenario.

Even with respect to the regulations it does impose, government is not necessarily at odds with business. A company that wishes to act ethically in international business may well find itself in competition with other companies from the same or from different nations that behave unethically when it is to their advantage to do so. If big enough and strong enough, the ethical company may nonetheless compete successfully. Yet it would prefer to have the rules the same for all. Since no company can control the actions of all other companies, a company of integrity may desire and lobby for national and international standards that make the rules of competition equal for all. In such cases, government may legislate what those companies that wish to compete ethically desire.

The interests of government and business thus often coincide, and the picture of government as the watchdog and regulator of business, of business and government on opposing sides, is a limited and partial one that hides other important relations.

Once these three myths have been exposed, the nature of the problem at stake of setting and abiding by standards in international business takes on a different dimension from previously. It is no longer an unachievable goal or a utopian enterprise.

International and global problems

No global executive authority does for the whole world what individual governments do or can do for their own countries. No global authority keeps international competition fair, in the sense of making and enforcing rules of competition that are the same for all. No global authority provides a safety net for those people or countries unable to compete successfully in the international market. No global authority either supplies or protects general or public goods, such as a livable environment, worldwide. Do we need such a global authority?

1. To some extent each government handles the task of keeping competition within its borders fair, although such regulation varies somewhat from system to system and country to country, sometimes in accord with internationally agreed upon standards and sometimes not. There is no need for uniform standards everywhere, and all the advanced industrial countries are capable of defending their own interests vis-a-vis other countries. The United States controls Japanese companies operating within its borders just as the Japanese control American companies. If either country acts in a way that the other considers unfair, each is able to defend its interests, apply pressures to negotiate change, and work for a mutually satisfactory resolution of the conflict. If the rules of one country are seen as unfavorable to external competition, other affected nations can, if they are in an equally strong position, retaliate. Such retaliation prompts the other party to reconsider its policies in the light of its broader interests and the international interactions it desires.

The situation is not the same with respect to multinational corporations from developed nations operating in less developed countries. Here the need for external regulation, such as the guidelines of the UN Commission on Transnationals, becomes important, as do industry guidelines such as those of the chemical industry. There is need to help such nations control exploitation and unfair practices by multinationals that violate basic ethical norms or internationally agreed upon guidelines. This may be provided by government-to-government assistance, by LDCs sharing information on successful means of control, or by industries or businesses informally policing themselves.

2. The second function of providing a safety net for those unable to compete is relegated almost entirely to national governments, with no system of transfer payments from nation to nation. Those with little have no recognized claim on those with much. Do rich countries have any obligation to poor countries? Do multinational corporations have any obligations in this area? The answer to both questions is yes. The problem is that thus far the only obligation that either countries or corporations acknowledge is one based on charity, especially in extreme emergencies or catastrophes. Articulating these obligations and devising a means for sharing the burden fairly and justly are pressing demands in this area that governments, the UN, and corporate or industry codes have not seriously addressed.

3. The third function, caring for the global common good, is presently handled by national governments and by international agreements. But there is no international government that oversees, regulates, coordinates, or enforces what is needed, for instance, to protect the global environment. Responsibility in this area cannot legitimately fall only on international business. The reason is not that business is operated for the self-interested purpose of profit maximization. It is rather that no single business is the cause and no single business can provide the remedy. Unless there is cooperative and almost full compliance with what is needed, the actions of individual firms make little difference.

Lack of full compliance and the desire of some companies to benefit from the actions of others without bearing any of the burdens (known as the free-rider problem) often give rise to legislation and governmental controls.[12] If we take the depletion of the ozone level as an example, no individual company has any incentive to limit its use of chlorofluorocarbons, if the alternatives are more expensive. They may do so for a variety of reasons. But unless all or most of those using these products desist, the ozone level continues to be adversely affected. Since so many different industries are involved, no single industry initiative will solve the problem. Individual nations can pass laws restricting the production and use of these items, but it is only by international cessation that the necessary results will be achieved. In this situation governments are the only effective means of achieving the required results. International agreement is necessary, and then international enforcement--such that those countries that do not control their emissions are somehow penalized either through trade or other sanctions by those countries that do control them. In some instances this may seem to be--or actually be--the large rich countries that have already done the damage imposing expensive alternatives on developing countries. That problem also has to be solved by negotiation.

Competition has played a more effective role in automotive safety than government regulation. For example, some auto manufacturers have introduced air bags prior to regulation as a selling point. Given the internationalization of markets and competition, once one company takes the lead in this regard, others not only in that country but throughout the world are pressured by the market to do likewise.

This shows the importance of leadership on the part of some companies and industries. *Noblesse oblige*. Setting higher standards than the existing norms takes imagination and courage. To be an example the company must somehow be visible, and that often means being a company that is large and is already an industry leader in productivity or quality of goods or market share. Whatever its size, leaders can by their actions set standards against which other companies are judged.

Global pluralism and common standards

On the global level there are many countries with many different structures and customs, needs, and aspirations. Can one set of standards apply to all? The answer depends on the standards and who determines them. No one country, no one firm can or should set the standards for all. Standards are appropriately set by those who will be affected by them. These include the firms affected, the countries, and the general public. Hence the importance of not ignoring what has already been negotiated, for instance, by the UN Commission on Transnational Corporations. There are two issues. One is the integrity of the firm or country or people. The other is the acceptance of norms or standards that involve others.

The pluralism worldwide means that there are different and sometimes conflicting standards.

If we preclude imposing standards on others, then the proper approach, given differences, is negotiation--and so compromise. The concept of compromise on ethical issues is often misunderstood. Each party comes to the bargaining table with its own set of principles, its own concept of justice, its own values. To be ethically acceptable by all, compromise is typically not about principles, concepts of justice, or values--even though agreement on principles is a philosopher's dream. What is essential is agreement on practices. Compromise on practices is the negotiator's and the diplomat's stock in trade, whether it be the result of negotiations carried on between businesses, between business and government, or between governments. Negotiation aims appropriately at practices that all parties can live with, given their principles, concepts of justice, and values. Only in this way can compromise be integrity-preserving.[13] And only in this way can there be binding agreements on practices that every party feels are just and acceptable, and so will be stable, because no party will have an incentive to undermine them.

Since it is easier to negotiate agreements when the parties have a great deal in common, it stands to reason that negotiations within, for instance, the EC will be hammered out before agreements between the EC and the Arab nations. It is more likely that agreement will be easier to achieve between Canada and the United States than between the United States and Japan. We can think of agreements taking place in concentric circles. In the inner circle are agreements between those countries or those businesses that have close links, ties, traditions, and history. Those serve as a basis for agreements with parties in the next broader concentric circle. These in turn form the basis for negotiating with those in the next ring, and so on until we come to the global level.

At each stage international negotiations may take place by governments, but it is understood that governments represent their interests, as well as hopefully the interests of their people, and the interests of business within their borders.

It is in the interest of countries that will be adversely affected by the depletion of the ozone level or by global warming to try to get everyone to act in concert to preclude these from causing increasing damage. But in fact each country is not interested in the abstract global common good but in the effects of everyone's actions on the environment insofar as they affect itself. If global warming affects some in a deleterious way and others in a positive way, getting joint action on the basis of the overall good is problematic. Similarly, if the economic development of some less developed countries is promoted by less environmental concern, it is not clearly to their advantage to observe standards advanced by developed countries. Negotiation will require that the less developed countries gain some advantage for accepting the additional costs that such protection involves. Nonetheless, within such countries multinationals from developed countries may be held to higher standards of pollution control than older indigenous companies as a condition of operating there. And some companies will voluntarily adhere to the higher standards as part of their policy, based on their own values and standards which they apply wherever they operate.

Government, business and the neglected third party

What then are the roles for business and government? It should be evident by now that clear lines of demarcation between the two are neither possible nor desirable. Sometimes business should take the lead, sometimes government, sometimes other groups. The situation in the countries of Central and Eastern Europe, recently emerging from collectivist socialism, are a case in point. In most instances the government has not yet been able to set norms for the emerging corporations and free enterprise transactions. Western corporations have the opportunity to help transmit and develop appropriate standards and to set an example of integrity in business. EC standards may be borrowed or adopted. Fledgling businesses may enunciate and develop justifiable standards on their own or in concert. The churches may preach moral norms that may be adopted. All of these should and probably will take place simultaneously. But there is no exclusively right way for the development of standards in this case.

Nonetheless any adequate answer to the question of the role of business and government in developing ethical standards must also acknowledge that this question omits an essential third party to the discussion, namely the people whom both business and government are intended to serve. Business and government always operate within a social and cultural context, which carry with them the norms and values, mores and morals, of the people of the country in question. Keeping this in mind, let me suggest some generalizations by way of a conclusion.

1.   The best starting point in the further development of standards for international business is self-regulation by business within the guidelines and standards that already exist. A general rule is that government should do only what business is unable or unwilling to do on its own.[14] Business is best suited to know where the potential for abuse lies. It is gratuitous to assume that all firms wish to exploit such potential. For if they did, the general public would sooner or later call for remedies. In some instances industries can and do set standards and police themselves. There is some danger, recognized in the United States by anti-trust laws, that self-regulation is open to abuses and collusion. Internationally, since we have no worldwide government, the dangers exist. Hence both nationally and internationally one cannot depend only on self-regulation by business. But government is not the only necessary body that sets standards. Also important are a variety of private bodies, media, enlightened consumers, vocal workers groups. When the conditions of competition are structurally unfair, then self-regulation does not work. Here the role of government enters. But just as there are unethical companies, there are also unethical governments. In these cases the subjugated, exploited, and abused people, other countries and governments, and other groups can provide some counterweight.

2.   Government is presently only national. There is no international government. Nonetheless, the need of controlling abuses by transnationals can be achieved by governments acting in concert. For instance, the BCCI scandal was an international one in which no government had adequate control over the banking industry worldwide, and so no government was able to prevent the abuses that took place. Secrecy in banking was part of the problem, and that is an issue that can be resolved in part by the banking industry and in part by the countries of the world agreeing on conditions under which

secrecy is not overriding. Any country that refuses to regulate the banking industry within its borders can be precluded from access to banks in other countries that agree to such standards.

International standards can be reached in a variety of ways: by a commission of the UN to which all concerned parties have access; by agreements among nations directly; by agreements and standards drawn up by the banking industry, with or without outside representation, such as the standards drawn up by the chemical industry. Other models--such as one involving model codes drawn up by groups or commissions composed of practitioners, governmental representatives, academic experts, and the general population--are possible. In any case, what any such group should do is start from what already exists in the way of standards both in the industry in question and in other areas. If the negotiations are not carried on government to government, then any model code or any code reached or presented must be adopted by individual countries. Only if all or most adopt them will they be effective worldwide. Those who refuse to adopt them, unless they can defend such refusal on reasonable ethical grounds--which will indicate a defect in the negotiation process or the end result--can appropriately be pressured to accept by public opinion, by refusal to do business in that area with that country, by government boycott, or by other means.

3. If seeing government and business in an adversarial relation is only part of the story, the fuller picture involves not only government and business but also what we can call in this context the neglected third party. This includes the media, which often serves as a watchdog, if it is not dominated and constrained by government or big business; the general public, in its capacity both as workers and as consumers; and the large number of intermediary groups in society, from unions and environmental and consumer groups to churches and Amnesty International, scholarly associations, grassroots movements, and specialized clubs.

Given the lack of enforcement internationally by an executive body, these intermediary groups become essential in the more informal enforcement of standards. Publicity, for instance, takes on a crucial role and is an effective tool in the enforcement of standards, provided that the people so informed of infractions are moved by the stories, the news, and the results of investigative reporting they receive. The media is the instrument that made known the Valdez spill and that publicized the Bhopal disaster. The media probed and brought to public attention the BCCI scandal. The positive role of the media is to encourage firms to abide by generally acknowledged or agreed upon standards, or face public exposure. The negative task is to uncover violations to expose. But unless there is a public that is interested and responsive to reports of violations, the media is ineffective.

Ethical standards adopted by firms are a reflection of ethical standards held by people.

The importance of public opinion and public pressure cannot be overstated. In the end these make the difference between standards that are respected and followed and those that are benignly ignored or allowed to atrophy.

The solution to acceptable international standards for business depends not only on business and government but on the many people that business and government serve. In the final analysis, people get both the business and the government that they demand and that, in a sense, they deserve.

References

1. By focusing attention on companies of integrity I am speaking to those firms that are already interested in acting ethically and in accordance with some standards. I suggest that that is the proper place to start, rather than with any attempt to convince unethical, amoral, or unprincipled companies that they should behave ethically. There is not only one set of rules, however, governing all firms that act with integrity, and different firms will emphasize different values consistent with their own history, home country, and corporate culture. For a discussion of personal integrity, see Martin Benjamin, *Splitting the Difference: Compromise and Integrity in Ethics and Politics*, Lawrence: University Press of Kansas, 1990, Chapter 3.

2. This myth parallels the Myth of Amoral Business in the United States, which I develop in *Business Ethics*, 3rd ed., New York: Macmillan, 1990, Chapter 1.

3. The cases of Michael Milken and Drexel Burnham in 1988 in the United States are well known. Among other reports, see James B. Stewart, "Scenes from a Scandal: The Secret World of Michael Milken and Ivan Boesky," *Wall Street Journal*, October 2, 1991, p. B1. On cases in Britain, see Gary Putka, "British Face Finance-Industry Scandals Just as They Move to Deregulate Markets," *Wall Street Journal*, August 12, 1985, p. 22. For a discussion of some of the cases in Japan, see James Sterngold, "Another Scandal in Japan, This Time Involving Billions," *The New York Times*, February 23, 1992, p. E3.

4. On the still evolving Maxwell story, see "An Honour System Without Honour," *The Economist*, December 14, 1991, pp. 81-82.

5. For a discussion of human rights as a basis for ethical standards and international business, see Thomas Donaldson, *The Ethics of International Business*, New York: Oxford University Press, 1989.

6. The exact number is difficult to determine, since different surveys define "codes" in different ways. The 1987 Conference Board

survey of 300 major corporations reports that 76% of such companies have written codes of conduct (*Corporate Ethics,* Research Report No. 900, p. 13). The number of companies adopting codes in countries other than the U. S. is still relatively small.

7. United Nations Economic and Social Council, E/1990/94, 12 June 1990, contains the "Proposed Text of the Draft Code of Conduct on Transnational Corporations." The Code is strongly criticized by some businesses. Since it is the product of negotiation, it is unlikely to completely satisfy everyone, all businesses, or all interests. For an overview and discussion of other codes see, John M. Kline, *International Codes and Multinational Business: Setting Guidelines for International Business Operations*, Westport, Conn.: Quorum Books, 1985.

8. Item 20(a) of the Code reads: "Transnational corporations shall refrain, in their transactions, from the offering, promising or giving of any payment, gift or other advantage to or for the benefit of a public official as consideration for performing or refraining from the performance of his duties in connection with those transactions." This would preclude the bribery of public officials, but not the paying of bribes to non-public officials.

9. See, *International Code of Breast-milk Substitutes*, Geneva: World Health Organization, 1981.

10. In 1984 Nestlé signed an agreement with the Infant Formula Action Coalition, which had sponsored a boycott of Nestlé products starting in 1977. In 1988 a group called Action for Corporate Accountability alleged violations of the Code and sought to renew the boycott, extending it to American Home Products Corp. as well (*New York Times*, Oct. 5, 1988, p. D2).

11. The ads appeared on April 11, 1990.

12. For a discussion of the free-rider problem in international business, see Manuel Velasquez, "International Business, Morality, and the Common Good," *Business Ethics Quarterly*, II (1992), pp. 27-40, with comments by John E. Fleming and Walter B. Gulick.

13. For a fuller discussion of compromise in ethics on international issues, see Richard T. De George, "Coherence and Ethics" (Presidential Address delivered before the Eighty-Eighth Annual Central Division Meeting of the American Philosophical Association, April 27, 1990), *Proceedings and Addresses of The American Philosophical Association*, 64 (1990), pp. 39-52. See also, Benjamin, *op. cit.*

14. This might be taken as an application of what is known in the Catholic tradition as the principle of subsidiarity. Although compatible with that principle, it does not depend on acceptance of it.

Part III

Religious Perspectives

9

Buddhism and Japanese Economic Ethics

Shunji Hosaka
and
Yukimasa Nagayasu

Introduction

Buddhism was initiated by Gautama Śiddhārtha (Śākyamuni Buddha) about four hundred years before the time of Jesus Christ, in the northern part of the Indian sub-continent now called Nepal. It is followed mainly in Asian nations. Buddha sought the final goal of life, and he came to the conclusion that it was "Nirvāṇa," the liberation from transmigration within the "Karmic world."

Buddhism is a comprehensive system of thought and practice, mainly consisting of the "Four Noble Truths" as follows:

1. *Suffering.* All human beings are suffering. This is one of the fundamental views of Buddhism about life in this world.

2. *Causality.* All suffering is caused by illusion and desire. This fact can only be understood by a kind of rational wisdom called "Prajñā".

3. *Salvation.* The realm free from suffering is Nirvāṇa, which is the true final goal of our life's journey. In Nirvāṇa, people can keep their lives free from the Karmic cycle and its suffering.

4. *Practice.* The only path to Nirvāṇa is the practice of "Precepts."

Buddhism, in short, regards human life in this world as a life of suffering, and it seeks to give people wisdom by which they can find the way of deliverance, not being caught by any attachment to life in this world.

P.M. Minus (ed.), *The Ethics of Business in a Global Economy.*

Theravāda Buddhism

Buddhism is not static, but quite dynamic, and has historically kept growing. As to the question of who can attain salvation and how, Buddhism gradually produced two answers, Theravāda and Mahāyāna Buddhism, the former of which is older and more conservative than the latter. Sharing the same goal of ultimate salvation, the two schools have significant differences in their scope and method.

Theravāda Buddhism expanded in South and Southeast Asia in places such as Sri Lanka, Thailand, and Myanmar. It holds to the classical and conservative traditions of Buddhism. Practitioners of this sect try to keep themselves away from this-world life. They consider that only monks who do not belong to the ordinary this-world life can attain Nirvāṇa and become free from the sufferings of the Karmic cycle. In Theravāda Buddhism, it is necessary for one to discard all possible social life, thus to renounce the mundane world and engage purely in religious practices.

Generally speaking, Buddhism in its early days did not refer to metaphysical affairs but exhorted people to follow the way to Nirvāṇa. There was no transcendental existence or creator, and people had no kind of Buddha image, such as an icon, for their worship. Buddhism was originally accepted as a moral or pragmatic religion, rather than a ritualistic one. This school of Buddhism recommended that people walk on the "Eight-Fold Noble Path" consisting of right view, right intent, right speech, right conduct, right livelihood, right endeavor, right memory, and right meditation.

Mahāyāna Buddhism

Out of this tradition a new school gradually grew, which came to be called Mahāyāna Buddhism and to be found in Northern and Eastern Asia, including Japan. It strongly advocates the attainment of "Bodhi" (Nirvāṇa), not only for special persons living as monks, but for "all sentient beings" who engage in religious practice based upon pure faith in the teachings of Buddhism, even as they continue to live within the mundane world. This school of Buddhism propagates the idea of living one's life according to the "Six Pāramitās," i.e., the six kinds of noble practice, as follows:

1. Dana-pāramitā: material and spiritual service to others.
2. Śila-pāramitā: practicing the precepts of pure life.
3. Kṣānti-pāramitā: perseverance in making efforts to live a correct life in this world.
4. Virya-pāramitā: assiduity in doing every kind of work.
5. Dhyāna-pāramitā: meditation to keep one's mind calm and pure, and to be grateful to benefactors.
6. Prajñā-pāramitā: the wisdom of looking at all things through Buddha's eyes, with warm and fair judgment.

Through such practice, the Buddha nature in every person's mind and body begins to grow towards the attainment of Nirvāṇa in this world. The main characteristics of such practice lie in the altruistic mind and conduct, which is called benevolence, "karuṇā maitṛi," and which serves all beings by taking away their suffering and giving them happiness.

While spreading among Asian people, Buddhism began to develop its own cosmology and metaphysics. Mahāyāna Buddhism's cosmology has had deep influence in Asia. It also has concepts of Hell and of a Land of the Highest Joy, which produced both a kind of fear to encourage people to avoid doing bad things, and also a hope for salvation in the next life.

Buddhism and economics in Japan

So far Buddhism has been highly developed in several Asian cultures. It may safely be said that one of its highest developments was attained in Japan. Along with the Japanese traditions of Shintoism, Confucianism, and Taoism, Buddhism has played an important role in the making of Japanese spiritual life.

The teachings and practice of Zen Buddhism, one of the highest forms of Buddhism, were the most suitable way for the spiritual training of the Samurai class who had to face death at any moment of their lives. Zen therefore took deep roots in the Japanese mind.

Having traditionally had a tendency to appreciate simplification, purity and non-abstractness, the Japanese people could successfully embody the spirit of Zen Buddhism in the forms of Do, such as Sa-Do (the tea ceremony) and Ka-Do (the flower arrangement). They thus transformed the abstract spirit of Buddhism into concrete performance. Here lies a universal role for Japanese Buddhism. It is to teach people how to purify and train their mental attitudes as well as their conduct in actual daily life.

In the tradition of Theravāda Buddhism, it is not so easy as in Mahāyāna Buddhism to develop an ethical perspective suitable for the modern economy, because the former school does not foster people's commitment to this world. But in Mahāyāna Buddhism it is natural to develop economic ethics in a positive way, and it encourages ordinary people to practice sincere work, production, commerce and consumption to help themselves and serve others. The basic point of such ethics is to engage oneself in the process of assiduous and incessant efforts, regarding every occupation as providing a venue for self-perfection.

Buddhist ethics in a global economy

In the view of Buddhism, all national economies are deeply suffering. Among advanced societies such as the European Community and the United States, a great number of people are now caught in the pecuniary lust of modern economic life. This is true also of Japan, albeit as a latecomer. In such situations, Buddhism is seemingly becoming weaker. But, in fact, it continues to be productive. Looked at from Buddhism's perspective, business ethics covers diversified fields from the micro to the global level, and from a minimum to a maximum level.

1. As for individuals, Buddhism teaches us how to think and behave in our work and consumption. We should regard any kind of work and consumption as a way to salvation. There is no difference of value in the kind of work as long as it results in social benefits. The point is that we should work in a spirit of benevolence, with true love for all beings, not only for human beings but also for other kinds of living beings and a-biotic substances.

2. Buddhism helps us open our spiritual eyes and encompass the global and ecological cycle. It teaches us how to maintain our lives without wasting precious resources, and how to control our desires, which is possible according to Buddhism's "Middle-Way" spirit applicable to production and consumption.

3. On the global level, the mainstream of present-day economics and people's this-worldly concepts regarding production and consumption are fundamentally problematic. The criteria of profit and maximum utility are dominant. But it is doubtful whether such thinking is suitable to conserve our planet. Buddhism's ethics contributes to the exploration of a new system of ecological economy. It leads us to transform our inner values in the direction of saving our planet from crisis. Non-selfishness in Buddhist ethics seems to be powerful enough to cope with global problems. We can say "non-selfishness is beautiful."

4. At the micro level of business, the corporation as an intimate community should respect all its members in a spirit of true mercy. Buddhism is non-aggressive. It makes people's minds self-reflective, gentle and peaceful by turning them to see things from a fresh and altruistic viewpoint beyond this selfish life, which comes from an understanding of the "emptiness and unreality of things."

5. Based upon the Buddhist view of change, i.e., "ever-change is unchanging," Buddhism can help people produce creative innovations. This view teaches that every being is, in a sense, undergoing the "entropy process." Here, technology and work are always in the process of collapse and creation, of creative change. The running water of a river never stops and never comes back again. Humankind can and must therefore keep constantly devising and developing new activities in our economic life.

6. By extending its attitude of ancestor worship and family love, Buddhism can contribute to the recovery of stability in our fluctuating industrial society. It can encourage us to turn our minds to taking care of subsequent generations by conserving human beings and all other beings as well. It shows us what the great family of all beings is, and should be, in the future on our planet. It may also be helpful for controlling world population. This is an "economy" which, from the Buddhist point of view, fundamentally means the harmony of all beings. Here is the common goal of all our cross-cultural discussions and actions.

10

A Jewish Perspective for Modern Business Morality

Meir Tamari

Wealth, greed and faith

Since the divine blueprint for the world is such that economic wants are satisfied through human endeavor in normal non-miraculous ways, there is nothing wrong or immoral with the possession of wealth and the acquisition of material goods. So, too, there is no spiritual value in poverty, nor is it a way to achieve spiritual redemption. The drive for economic wealth is morally legitimate and an essential prerequisite for the existence and welfare of the human race.

Yet at the same time, since greed is so powerful and all-pervasive, that drive can result in widespread unethical behavior and great economic immorality, leading to injustice and oppression. This greed is enhanced and empowered by man's perpetual fear of economic uncertainty. So we perpetually seek to protect ourselves against the risks involved in the market and in the human condition, through legitimate means but also by immoral ones.

In a world where men know that the full extent of their future needs and the source of satisfying them are assured, there would be no need for fraud, exploitation, or business immorality. Faith in Divine Providence and the assurance that God provides for all needs, frees man from the necessity to find unethical ways to protect himself from uncertainty or to deny private property rights of others for the same purpose. At the same time, it is this faith which allows people to take the risks needed for entrepreneurial development, thus maintaining the legitimate search for wealth within moral parameters.

P.M. Minus (ed.), *The Ethics of Business in a Global Economy.*

The belief that all wealth originates from God, that God's bounty—rather than luck, hard work or ability—is the real source of our economic success, is the only reliable means whereby greed is able to be channelled into morality. Mere exhortations to morality or personal decisions based on changing individual concepts of ethics are only of limited value. At the same time, because economic drive is so powerful and pervasive a force, legislated morality is essential; otherwise society is left only with good intentions. The legislation needed to provide the ethical parameters for business activity cannot function, however, without a deep-rooted and commonly accepted normative morality.

Economic immorality

The divine origin of wealth mandates that it not be earned through immoral or unjust ways. Even where they are legal, therefore, exploitation, misuse of power, undisclosed conflicts of interest and oppression through withheld information cannot coexist with a God-given morality. So, Judaism rejects the concept of "let the buyer beware," and places the onus for full disclosure on the seller. The biblical injunction against placing a "stumbling block in the path of the blind" is understood as forbidding giving advice or selling goods and services that are to the physical or spiritual detriment of the other party.

Moreover, most economic crimes are committed in secret and so are a rejection of God's ability to see and know all. In this perspective, robbery is taken out of its context of violent crime and is seen as including acts such as the denial of debts incurred, the private use of another's property or money placed in one's trust, and withholding wages. The social or personal pressure on people to agree to transactions to which they are opposed, as sometimes happens in hostile takeovers, is considered to be coercion and therefore tantamount to robbery. Above all, the spiritual damage to the performer of unethical acts has always to be considered, over and above the financial damage suffered by the victim. This makes avoidance of immoral acts even when they are legally possible essential to one who considers himself a Godfearing person.

Mutual assistance

God as the Provider and Father of all men is the source of the brotherhood of man. The world consists, therefore, not only of vertical relationships between man and God but also horizontal relationships between man and man. Mankind is not just a mass of unrelated beings but a large family linked by their Creator. The wealth provided therefore by God, although meant primarily for the satisfaction of the needs and wants of the private owner, is also meant to be used to satisfy the needs of the poor and the inefficient—the old, the weak and even the lazy. Just as business morality needs to be legislated, so too does this mutual assistance. If left to the philanthropy of the individual and to his acts of kindness, human nature and the lust for wealth would limit this act of sharing. So society acquires a property right in the wealth of the individual to provide, through compulsory acts of taxation, the social and charitable needs to its members. These funds are either Tzedaka—Charity, or Tzedek—Justice. Voluntary sharing of wealth in response to the claims of the poor and weak are charity, but compulsory participation in the communal funds to provide these needs is an act of justice. Non-participation in such funding becomes tantamount to theft, either from the recipients of the funding or from the other participants who now have to provide a greater share. This divine insistence on using part of private wealth for the needs of others makes it holy money, which also demands that it be neither wasted nor abused.

Mankind is the pinnacle of creation, hence all natural resources exist to provide for the human race. This makes the use of these resources legitimate and necessary, yet at the same time, it limits their exploitation. Since they are granted to us in a custodial relationship, they may not be frivolously dissipated nor wantonly destroyed, even where the legal ownership is unquestioned. So the Rabbis likened one who wastes his property or destroys it in anger to an idolater, for both deny the divine source of wealth. Man as a custodian of natural resources needs to husband them, so that in addition to being used, they remain for future generations. In this, he becomes, as it were, a partner in the divine process of creation. Society may need to limit its economic development in order to allow for that and to earn the spiritual and social benefits of environmental health.

The moral corporation

While Judaism recognizes the limited liability corporation as a legitimate form of business organization, it applies it only to the rights of the creditors. This form of organization limits the claims of the creditors to the equity of the firm and protects the personal assets of the shareholders. Since this protection is public knowledge, there is nothing unethical or immoral about it. However, the corporation cannot be used by the shareholders or by the directors as a shield behind which unethical behavior may be conducted. Judaism places the same demands on the corporation as it does on the individual. Directors cannot claim that they are only doing the bidding of their shareholders, since Judaism does not permit one to be an agent for an immoral act. They cannot argue that their sole duty is to maximize the profits of their shareholders, since Judaism limits in many ways everybody's right to maximize profits.

So, too, the shareholders cannot free themselves from claims against their private assets for damages caused by the corporation, since it is their wealth that caused the damage. Being the owners of the corporation obligates them to all the social obligations that Judaism places on the individual regarding the physical safety of their employees, abuse of the environment, dishonesty in trading, etc. Indeed, there are instances where the corporate form is able to discharge these obligations far more efficiently than is the individual. Maimonides ranks giving a man a job or lending him money to establish his own firm as the highest form of charity. Corporations would seem to be implementing Maimonides by making their facilities available to their discharged employees for retraining, or part of their funds as interest-free loans for redundant workers to become self-employed, or even by simply providing information as to job possibilities.

"Economics of enough"

The wide-ranging Jewish framework for moral economic behavior that flows from recognition of the divine source of wealth ultimately leads to an "economics of enough." Every Jew, irrespective of age, social status, wealth or intellect, is obligated to study Torah, the revealed law of God. This obligation is one unlimited by time, so that it severely curtails the "free" time available for economic activity and, therefore, for the accumulation of wealth. In addition, both the religious milieu of Judaism and its communal living pattern have contributed, over the ages, to an ingrained modesty in demand. If adhered to, this modesty substantially dampens the individual's demand for a spiraling standard of living and leads thereby to a reduced pressure to find immoral ways to satisfy it. To the classical economic axiom that "more is better than less," Judaism would provide the rejoinder of the Patriarch Jacob: "I have all I need."

11

Christianity and Business Ethics

Jack Mahoney

Ethical implications of foundational beliefs

The Christian religion follows the Hebrew Bible in adopting a positive view of physical and human creation, and in envisaging God as deeply concerned with how human creatures behave ethically towards each other. It also believes that God entered into history in the person of Jesus of Nazareth to save humanity from the self-inflicted wounds of sin and to introduce a new era in which humanity would come to share God's own life in mutual love, harmony and justice. Christianity is thus centrally concerned with beliefs about *creation*, *sin*, *salvation* and *completion*, and with their ethical implications.

Christians can place particular emphasis on one or other of these beliefs in a way that shapes their attitude to human behavior, including business behavior. Thus, concentrating on God's bringing humanity to *completion* can give rise to two contrasting basic attitudes towards the present life. One views it as of little significance compared to the life to come, and consequently avoids becoming immersed to any great extent in the affairs of this passing world, including business. The other views God's work of completion as already in progress, and aims to cooperate in it by striving to create more just economic and social conditions that will enable all the peoples of God's earth to live even now lives worthy of their destiny.

Both these attitudes to the work of divine completion regard society as falling short of what it will be, or of what it could now be, as a result of human *sin*, which many Christians also view as the outstanding characteristic of society, including the realm of business.

P.M. Minus (ed.), *The Ethics of Business in a Global Economy*.

This great emphasis on sin would lead to despair of humanity, were it not for the Christian belief in *salvation*: God's gracious mercy in bringing forgiveness and hope through the death and new life of Jesus Christ. Many Christians interpret this as meaning not just that Christ has saved humanity, but that humanity continually needs to be saved, and forgiven, for its inherent self-centeredness, its proud trust in its own resources, and its proneness to succumb to the allurements of worldly goods and worldly success, of which occupation in business is considered a conspicuous example.

Other Christians believe either that sin is not so prevalent, or that Christ's work of saving and healing humanity is proving effective. Consequently they stress the fourth belief in the goodness of *creation*, and in the basic trustworthiness even now of human beings and of human enterprise and motivation. They thus recognize the positive nature of many occupations in society and view the conduct of business as a cooperating with God in the creative work of developing the earth's and humanity's resources for the common benefit of all.

The challenge for Christians themselves is to give due weight to each of these basic beliefs, and to address to business on the one hand words of encouragement and approval for what it is capable of doing and to some degree actually is doing, and on the other hand words of criticism and impatience for what it is not doing or not yet doing sufficiently. This is summed up in acknowledging *a continuing moral tension for business between the God-given goal of humans cooperating to develop the earth's resources for their common well-being, and the historical reality of a human liability to pursue individual interests at the expense of others and thus frustrate the ultimate purpose of God's work of creation.*

The ultimate goal: shared human well-being

The importance of shared human well-being as the ultimate goal of society, and of business, is highlighted for Christians by their further belief in the fact and the challenge of *human solidarity*. God's enterprise of creation, salvation and completion is viewed as one which encompasses humanity as a whole. The moral commandment to be found in Judaism and singled out by Jesus, to love one's neighbor, placed no conditions on who is to qualify as neighbor—unless it be those particularly who are most in need. Christianity thus opposes any view of society that depends on or leads to elitism, alienation, or adversarialism. It also de-absolutizes political, social, and economic structures against its criterion of a shared human destiny and shared access to the fruits of God's creation for all the earth's inhabitants. It thus sees it incumbent on society to ensure that economic theories to produce material wealth are not regarded as ends in themselves, and to contrive that whatever success they produce is not gained for some of its members to the ultimate social detriment of their fellows. Hence also, quite apart from any ethical duties of legal compliance, it views business as obliged to acknowledge the human purpose of social measures to regulate its activities, and to accept any other moral conclusions affecting its behavior to which the fact and the challenge of human solidarity appear to lead.

Yet Christianity also stresses the profound significance of *individuals*, not as interchangeable units of humanity but as possessing an inalienable dignity based on each being a unique creature of God and a sister or brother of Jesus Christ. This has consequences, not only for the way in which humans ought to treat and respect each other in all their dealings, but also for the contributions which individuals as such have to offer their fellows in all their social undertakings, including the conducting of business.

An important belief that many Christians today find appealing and encouraging expresses this individual potential in terms of *vocation*, or the unique "call" which individuals receive personally to serve God within the particular way of life in which they find themselves. This belief in a worldly vocation recognizes the value and potentiality of many social occupations to provide a context for individuals to devote themselves to God by pursuing their calling with diligence and simplicity, an attitude which historically came to be termed the "Protestant work ethic" and which may have contributed to the development of capitalism. It also enables believers to invest their public and professional activities with the religious motive and response of serving others, as the practical working out of the command to love one's neighbor and to follow the example of Christ who spent his life in service of his fellows.

The individual and society

Contemporary Christian reflection also proposes two ways in which the relationship and the tension that is often experienced between the individual and society can be positively expressed and advanced, with consequences for social conduct, including the conduct of business. One develops the biblical idea of *covenant* as a model for human relationships. The bonding initiated by God with representative individuals in history and with the people of Israel and, as Christians believe, renewed afresh with humanity in Jesus Christ, inculcates a view of human existence in the created universe, and a view of the universe itself, as gifts from God to be received in gratitude, to be held in mutual promise and trust, and to be administered and developed in joint responsible stewardship. Relationships between humans as part of the creative and saving work of God are also viewed as ideally covenantal, not as an area for convenience, exclusive self-interest and destructive rivalry, but as a partnership of solidarity and mutual regard based on a shared pledge and commitment to a common purpose.

The consequence of such an approach to business relationships is to invest them with a quality and a texture richer than purely contractual or legal compliance, and to introduce human and relational factors of which the terminology of stakeholders is only a pale expression.

The other modern Christian approach to promoting a positive relationship between society and the individual explores the nature of human *personhood* as offering a bridge between the two. Western philosophical traditions have stressed the distinctiveness of human individuals to vindicate their social, political and economic independence, but they have worked in a social vacuum that takes no account of the possibility of relationships that express not just human dependence or independence, but the richer quality of human interdependence. Similarly, life in society provides individuals with the occasion and often the need to claim various human rights, yet it also provides a balancing context of social responsibility for the exercise of such rights.

This human characteristic of individuals interacting positively in community is what a modern understanding of the idea of person claims to express. It acknowledges the importance of community support and structures for the development and flourishing of individuals, while also recognizing the value of individuals in contributing to the maintenance and prosperity of the community that they share.

One major consequence for business that follows from thus understanding the idea of the human person as richer than that of the human individual, to include the human disposition to live and work together, involves recognizing and encouraging, and never suppressing, the contributions that individuals can uniquely and valuably make, including their moral insights, when all are engaged in various capacities in a common enterprise.

Toward a dialogue between Christianity and business

The challenging and comprehensive contribution of Christianity to the ethical conduct of business is not the delivery of a series of arbitrary moral injunctions. It is an exploring within the realm of business of the practical consequences of those beliefs about God and humanity that Christians hold as their distinctive way of interpreting and construing human existence. It unashamedly asks ultimate questions about the purpose of life and of human society, and about the intrinsic purpose of business as one among many expressions of social relationships and activities. It also claims to offer answers to such questions in ways that do not just satisfy intellectual curiosity, but that have, as has been shown, behavioral implications for business activity at all levels.

In its turn, business can address to Christianity a series of challenges as part of its contribution in a potentially fruitful dialogue. One is to enquire to what extent Christians themselves live up to the exacting ethical standards that their religion proclaims, and this not simply in legalistic compliance but as persons of character and integrity imbued with a noble and joyous vision and task for humanity. Another challenge to Christians is to scrutinize the claims for the truth, and the practicability and the adaptability, of their vision and beliefs as these apply to business. For Christianity is not a static collection of timeless beliefs and once-for-all moral conclusions, but a living and developing tradition of interaction between beliefs and contemporary experience that seeks to clarify and to do justice to both. A third challenge to Christians is to explore what common aims and what shared moral ground and values they may have with their fellows in society who subscribe to no religion or who espouse another. For if the Christian "gospel" claims, as it does, to be "good news" for all human beings, including those engaged in business, it is surely important that all concerned share in that news to the greatest extent and in the greatest measure possible.

12

Business Ethics in Islam

M. Cherif Bassiouni

A universal message

Islam's holistic approach is evident in three essential tenets: the unity of God, the unity of humankind, and the unity of religion. Because of these tenets, Islam is deemed universal and timeless; as such, it applies to all peoples and in all places. Islam is not a new religion but the continuation of divine revelations from Abraham to Mohammed, the last of the prophets. The *Qur'àn* explicitly states that it is the continuation and conclusion of the Creator's religion given to humankind.

The *Shari'à*, or the law of Islam, is based on the *Qur'àn*. Probably the most encompassing and most universal ethical prescription of the *Shari'à* is contained in a verse of the *Qur'àn* which requires the Muslim, at all times and in all circumstances, to act in what can be translated from Arabic as a decent and benevolent way, and to refrain from wrongdoing. This overall guiding conception is reminiscent of Aristotle's admonishment not to harm others and to deal with others as one would wish to have others deal with oneself. The well-known "golden rule" of the New Testament, "Do unto others as you would have them do unto you," is echoed in Islam, "No one of you is a believer until he desires for his brother that which he desires for himself." Buddhism expresses it in terms of "Hurt not others in ways that you yourself would find hurtful." The Judaic rule is: "What is hateful to you, do not to your fellow man. That is the entire law; all the rest is commentary." This basic message of the one and only Creator thus is found in all His revelations to His one humankind.

P.M. Minus (ed.), *The Ethics of Business in a Global Economy*.

Beyond this fundamental teaching that is shared with other great ethical traditions, the *Shari'à* regulates almost every aspect of relationships, ranging from that which is between the Creator and humankind, to intimate matters of interpersonal relations. Because the *Shari'à* is a comprehensive legal system which regulates all aspects of society, rules of interpretation acquire a prominent position, and techniques of legal interpretation, based on the different schools of jurisprudence, are paramount. A variety of contrasting positions and schools of thought has developed among Muslims across the centuries.

Commerce and business

Through all that variety, commerce and business have remained central subjects in the Islamic ethical tradition. During a limited period of Islam's history, its spread was due to the sword, but otherwise its spread has been essentially through individual proselytization, more particularly as a result of trade and commerce. Because Arabs historically had a tradition of trade and commerce, when they became Muslims they continued that tradition. It was due to their superiority in navigation, shipbuilding, astronomy and scientific measuring devices that Arab and Muslim commerce and trade developed and reached so many peoples throughout the world. Furthermore, the Muslim world, certainly during its first few centuries, was at the crossroads of the ancient trade routes from the Mediterranean, the Arabian Gulf, East Africa, and the Indian subcontinent, all the way to China. As a result of this particular trading relationship, a significant number of Arab words relating to trade and commerce have found their way into Western languages. But, Muslim traders could not have propagated the faith if it were not for their strong adherence to what is now called "business ethics."

The dominant Arab culture, which characterized the early centuries of Islam, has since lost its influence over customary business practices, and it has been replaced by the influence and conditioning factors of diverse civilizations and cultures.

Islam is estimated to have over one billion adherents in almost every country in the world. Though popular beliefs link Islam to the Arab world, in fact there are only a hundred and twenty million Muslims living in the Arab world, the cradle of that faith.

Most Muslims are found in Asia and Africa, but a growing minority of Muslims now resides in Western Europe and North America.

Teachings about economic practice

In the absence of unified legislative and judicial authorities among Muslims, practices differ and enforcement is practically non-existent. This diversity among Muslims has generated different customs, behavior, and expectation in business relations. Generally, however, Islamic economic and business conceptions are very much the equivalent of a free-enterprise, private-sector market economy approach, though they do not exclude the right of society to impose limitations for the greater benefit of the community. The *Shari'à* recognizes the right to private property but retains the community's right to what may be called "eminent domain" or other collective interests. Private property is enshrined in the *Shari'á*. In fact, one of the important ethical considerations in property is that its use is permissible, but abuse and waste are forbidden.

In a *Hadith*, the prophet says that nine-tenths of all the bounty of God, which includes income, is derived from commerce. To a large extent, this explains the drive of Muslims over the centuries to meet their economic needs through commerce and to consider profits as not only legitimate, but a desirable way of engaging in human industry. Profits are very much part of the activities of Muslims, if they are obtained in a permissible way. However, profits cannot overshadow other duties of brotherhood, solidarity, charity, and they are, of course, subject to *Zakat*, which is a particular tax imposed upon Muslims.

The *Shari'à* divides rules of conduct between *Halal* and *Haram*, meaning essentially that which is permissible and that which is impermissible. The general rule is that which is not explicitly or implicitly impermissible is therefore permissible. The distinction between the *Halal* and the *Haram* applies to legitimate and illegitimate profits. The illegitimate profit is particularly exemplified by *riba*, which is to a large extent the equivalent of usury. However, it also has come to mean the collection of a predetermined fixed amount of interest. The Muslim is allowed to earn a profit only from his work or, if his capital is involved, whenever he shares the risk of loss. Consequently, gambling is prohibited, as is undue profiting from the need or misery of others.

The gray area between gambling and speculation or high business risk is open to debate, depending upon whether one follows a rigid dogmatic approach or a liberal one. A specific example is buying stock in a company, which is *Halal*; consequently, buying stock through a market is an extension thereof. But does that permissible extension cover stock market speculation? Some modern liberal scholars rely on a subjective criterion to answer the question, namely the intention of the investor to distinguish between legitimate risk-taking and illegitimate gambling. They believe that in the final analysis, only the Almighty can judge such intentions. But, dogmatists would objectively look at the activity and determine whether it reasonably appeared to be in the nature of gambling because it is excessively speculative, or is legitimate because it is a permissible high-risk venture.

Nothing, however, prohibits income derived from what would be equivalent to mutual funds or special trust earnings or other contemporary forms of financing investments, where the investor shares in the profits and also bears the burden of potential loss. This is the basis of modern Islamic banks, which operate, or are supposed to operate, as mutual funds, even though their activities extend to traditional banking.

The obligations of piety

In one of the verses of the *Qur'àn*, Chapter 2, Verse 177, it is said:

> "It is not righteousness that you turn your faces towards East or West; but it is righteousness to believe in God and the last day, and the angels and the Book, and the messengers; to spend of your substance, out of love for Him, for your kin, for orphans, for the needy, for the wayfarer, for those who ask, and for the ransom of slaves; to be steadfast in prayer, and practice regular charity; to fulfill the contracts which you have made."

Thus, contracts are the most important bond that exists between Muslims, as well as between Muslims and non-Muslims. In a *Hadith* of the prophet, it is said:

> "The buyer and the seller have the option (of canceling the contract), as long as they have not separated; then, if they both speak the truth and make it manifest, their transaction shall be blest, and if they conceal and tell lies, the blessing of their transaction shall be obliterated."

The prophet goes on to say:

> "The truthfulest, honest merchant is with the prophet and the truthful ones and the martyrs."

Thus, the fulfillment of obligations in good faith and in accordance with principles of "business ethics" is not only required; it is inseparable from the general obligation of piety.

A Muslim's word is his strongest bond. That is particularly significant because a Muslim may be called upon to take the oath before a court or arbitration, which is the usual way of informal settlement of disputes. That oath is outcome determinative, particularly with respect to non-Muslims, whose oath is not deemed to have the same evidentiary weight as the Muslim's. The reason is that the Muslim incurs the wrath of God if he perjures himself.

Fulfillment of obligations also includes the notion of rectitude, which includes rejection of taking undue advantage of another. Fairness is deemed both a means and an end, irrespective of the practical realities, and honesty is not a virtue, but an expected trait in every Muslim.

These qualities and characteristics are particularly significant because the Prophet Mohammed was a merchant who exhibited them. His life is the example to follow.

Fifteen centuries ago Islam was a spiritual, social, and legal revolution. Its potential for effecting progress in a positive way remains unchanged. This is essentially the belief of enlightened liberal Muslims who do not have a regressive view of religion and history. Indeed, at the height of its civilization, between the seventh and twelfth centuries, Islam was neither repressive nor regressive. On the contrary, it was a progressive, humanistic, and legalistic force for reform and justice. But this original thrust cannot be seen in the contemporary practices of Muslim societies, proving once more that religion and law are instruments of social policy. Religion and law are only as true to their higher purposes as are those who shape social policy.

Muslim scholars of all tendencies do not consider Islam to be an evolving religion, but rather a religion and legal system whose application to all times necessarily requires evolution. Indeed, the provisions of the *Qur'àn* are such that by their disciplined interpretation, Islam can provide the solution to contemporary economic and social problems in Muslim societies.

Part IV

Six Business Cases

WESTWOOD, INC.*

Case Summary

Your firm imports hardwoods from tropical rain forests. The company was attacked by radical environmentalists who object to the marketing of your most lucrative product.

General Discussion Questions

1. Is there a socially responsible way for a company to market environmentally important hardwoods from tropical rain forests?

2. What are the dangers of companies giving in to special interest groups?

3. What obligations does a company have to ensure that the environment is not being harmed by the practices of its suppliers in foreign locations?

* Adapted by Karen Marquiss and Joanne B. Ciulla from "Tropical Plywood Imports, Inc.," LaRue Tone Hosmer © Columbia University Graduate School of Business, 1991.

WESTWOOD, INC.

Ten years ago, you joined Westwood, Inc. as its Chief Executive Officer. The firm imports a number of hardwoods from various parts of the world and sells them on the domestic market. During your tenure, the company has grown from a small startup enterprise to a firm whose sales exceed $800 million per annum.

Now, after years of hard work, the company faces a formidable threat from stockholders and local environmentalist groups who have become outraged over the company's role in the destruction of the world's tropical rain forests. Last night, a radical group known as the Green Coalition set off a bomb in company headquarters. Fortunately, the explosion injured no one, but the ensuing fire destroyed several offices and demolished some vital company documents.

Knowing that the situation has reached a critical point, you call an emergency meeting of your top advisers. Included in the group are the company founder and several other members of the Board of Directors. You solicit their advice on what actions you should take to resolve the problem.

Westwood's most profitable commodity is a plywood product made from meranti, a tropical hardwood that grows plentifully throughout Indonesia. Westwood sells about $525 million of meranti plywood annually (over 65% of total revenues) to lumber yards and industrial firms. The firm constitutes one of four major corporations in the region that purchase meranti.

Because of its strong dense consistency, meranti makes an ideal plywood. The wood has no growth rings and can be cut into very thin veneers and then laminated into 1/4-inch sheets. The plywood makes excellent concrete forms at a very low cost. It can easily be cut, drilled and nailed without danger of splitting. Builders use less wood overall than with other products since meranti is sold in such thin layers. Manufacturers also use the hardwood for kitchen cabinets and paneling in travel trailers and mobile homes.

Meranti gives Westwood a strong competitive edge in the plywood market. Locally-grown softwoods such as fir and spruce tear very easily at the soft inner portion of the ring, so plywood produced from these woods must be a minimum of 3/8 inch thick. At the same time, producers reserve more expensive hardwoods such as maple, cherry or walnut for fine furniture. While a few comparable hardwoods are available in other parts of the world, meranti remains the cheapest and most cost-effective source for Westwood's plywood products.

Despite meranti's good qualities, the company had come under an increasing degree of scrutiny because of its association with this product. The concern over worldwide rain forest depletion grew from a handful of concerned shareholders six or seven years ago to a groundswell of protest in recent months. Angry members of the Green Coalition, complete with picket signs and jeers, greeted company employees each morning as they arrived at Westwood's headquarters. Several days ago, a block of shareholders, all members of the local chapter of the Green Coalition, sold their shares in protest, and placed the Westwood name on the Green's "Environmental Blacklist."

Your managers ascribed this recent surge in environmental activism to an article published in a leading national newspaper the prior week. The article reported that scientists now believe the rain forests are being destroyed at a rate greater than the annual losses earlier reported by government agencies. Recent surveys taken by satellite revealed that each year 40 million acres of rain forest simply disappear.

Experts estimated that Indonesia loses over 2 million acres of tropical forest per year, surpassed only by Brazil and India (See Table 1). Officials called the destruction of the rain forest "one of the worst ecological disasters of the 20th century." If not halted, the practice could potentially lead to shortages of natural resources, global warming, mass extinction of indigenous species, and suffering for the displaced tribal people who live in the forests.

Your advisers also remind you that scientists have yet to prove the validity of the greenhouse effect. Furthermore, company policy dictates that all timber must be harvested in a selective logging method in which the meranti trees must reach at least 20 inches in diameter before they are cut. Westwood allows no clear-cutting, leaving the smaller trees for future harvests, up to 35 years from now. This minimizes the destruction of endangered species, conserves natural resources for future use, and allows native populations to continue to dwell in the forests. Nevertheless, critics were quick to point out that the lumber harvested for Westwood had covered a 200,000-acre area in the past 2 years alone.

128

No one from Westwood has ever visited the meranti logging sites in Indonesia. The company relies entirely upon assurances from Indonesian government officials who own the land and oversee the harvest. Over the years, Westwood has maintained a mutually rewarding relationship with the regime. Cutting the meranti trees helps provide jobs and income for the local people and simultaneously furnishes the domestic market with a very useful and profitable commodity.

At the end of the discussion, several top managers and one member of the board concede that Westwood should withdraw from the meranti market, others disagree. Your advisers are clearly divided on the issue.

Table 1
Estimated Versus Actual Losses in Tropical Forest Acreage*

Nation	Annual Acreage Losses Estimated 1981-1985	Annual Acreage Losses Revealed in Satellite Survey 1988
Brazil	3,657,000	19,768,000
Cameroon	198,000	247,000
Costa Rica	160,000	306,000
India	363,000	3,707,000
Indonesia	1,482,000	2,224,000
Myanmnar (Burma)	254,000	1,673,000
Philippines	227,000	353,000
Thailand	437,000	981,000
Vietnam	161,000	427,000
Totals	6,939,000	29,686,000

*Source: World Resource Institute, reported in the *New York Times*, June 8, 1990, p. A10.

THE QUANDARY AT PUREDRUG*

<u>Case Summary</u>

You are the Chief Executive Officer of an international pharmaceutical concern. Faced with sagging corporate profits and declining market share, you must make a difficult decision concerning the export of a new lucrative medication to the Philippines.

<u>General Discussion Questions</u>

1. Is it ethical for a company to have one standard of safety in its home country and a lower standard of safety in a developing country?

2. Who has the ethical obligation to determine acceptable levels of risk, the seller or the buyer?

3. Does the seller have an ethical obligation to make sure that the buyer understands all of the risks associated with a product?

---

*   Adapted by Karen Marquiss and Joanne B. Ciulla from "Dorrence Corporation Tradeoffs," Hans A. Wolf
    © Columbia University Graduate School of Business, 1991.

THE QUANDARY AT PUREDRUG

You are the Chief Executive Officer of Puredrug, a large pharmaceutical company with sales and operations throughout the world. Your firm has an outstanding reputation for quality as well as a long-term record of growth and profitability. Over the past 10 years, sales grew at an average annual compound rate of 12 percent and profits increased by an average of 15 percent per annum. The company had not experienced losses since 1957, and stock prices remained consistently healthy.

In spite of Puredrug's impeccable record, by October 1991 your company is in trouble. Due to a general economic downturn and a few product development problems, the firm faces a declining market share and weakened corporate profits. Although still profitable, Puredrug fell far short of its goals established for 1990. As of the end of the third quarter of 1991, you project a $4 million loss for the year. The value of your corporate stock has already dropped by one-fifth of its 1990 year-end value, and a loss for the year could result in an even more substantial devaluation. Small investors might switch to pharmaceutical companies with better results. Even worse, a disappointing year could cause large institutional investors such as pension funds to support a takeover by one of your competitors.

In an attempt to remedy the immediate situation, you call an emergency meeting of your top managers to poll their suggestions. Charles Dunn, head of the International Export Division, reminds you that his department has an opportunity to sign an $8 million contract with the Philippine government. The contract involves the sale of Travolene, a new injectable drug, developed by Puredrug for the treatment of serious viral infections, including measles. The drug remains difficult and expensive to manufacture and has been in very short supply since its introduction. The 1991 budget did not include this sale due to the lack of product availability.

Dunn mentions that at this time Puredrug's inventory contains a large lot of Travolene, produced at a cost of about $2 million. The government rejected the batch for the domestic market on the basis of a new, very sensitive test for endotoxin. The authorities recently adopted this test in addition to the standard method that had been used for many years. The more sensitive test revealed a very low level of endotoxin in the batch of Travolene, while the old procedure uncovered no endotoxin whatsoever.

You ask Ann Doe, the company's Chief Medical Safety Officer, whether this rules out shipping the batch to the Philippines. She explains that the Philippines and many other countries still rely exclusively on the old test. Ann said, "It always takes them awhile to adopt more sophisticated practices, and sometimes they never do. Endotoxin might cause high fever when injected into patients, but I can't tell you that the level in this batch is high enough to cause trouble. Still, how can we have a double standard, one for our nation and one for Third World countries?"

Charles Dunn interrupts, "It's not our job to over-protect other countries. The health authorities in the Philippines know what they are doing. Our officials always take an extreme position. Measles is a serious illness. Last year in the Philippines half of the children who contracted measles died. It's not only good business but also good ethics to send them the only batch of Travolene we have available."

As the other senior members of Puredrug's management begin to take sides on the issue, you contemplate your options. In the short run, the profit margin on the lot of Travolene would boost Puredrug's bottom line into the black for the year. In addition, the sale to the Philippines could foster a lucrative long-term relationship and lead to expansion into other Asian markets.

You leave the meeting with an uneasy feeling. You have only 72 hours before you must present a plan to Puredrug's Board of Directors.

THE OIL RIG*

Case Summary

You are the new C.E.O. of an oil exploration and drilling firm. To streamline operations, you decide to visit each of your offshore oil rigs. On your first visit to an outfit off the coast of Africa, you discover a mini-society where segregation is a way of life.

General Discussion Questions

1. What kinds of inequality are intolerable in an organization?

2. Whose standards of health and safety should a company use in a developing country?

3. Is the value of human life the same in all cultures?

---

*   Adapted by Karen Marquiss and Joanne B. Ciulla from "The Oil Rig," a Wharton student case.

THE OIL RIG

You have just taken over as the new Chief Executive Officer of Stratton Oil Company, an exploration and drilling firm under contract to a major multinational oil company. Your enterprise has experienced ups and downs over the last few years due to the fluctuation of international oil prices and complications with overseas operations.

Many of the operational problems stem from difficulties with Stratton's offshore oil drilling rigs. Maintenance and equipment costs have skyrocketed. You have received several reports of strained labor relations on the platforms. One incident caused such an uproar that the rig manager halted operations for over a week. In addition, there have been a number of complaints from conscientious shareholders concerned with the environmental impact of these rigs.

In an attempt to address these issues, you decide to get a first-hand look at the offshore drilling operations. On your first excursion, you visit a rig off the coast of Africa, dubbed the "Voyager 7." You discover that an oil rig is really a small society, separate and distinct from the rest of the world.

Stratton's Voyager 7 is a relatively small "jack-up" (a platform with legs) with dimensions of about 200 feet by 100 feet. The platform houses a crew of 150 men, made up of skilled laborers, "roustabouts" or unskilled laborers, maintenance staff, and 30 expatriates. The expatriates work as roughnecks, drillers, technicians or administrators. The top administrator on the Voyager 7 is the "tool pusher," an expatriate who wields almost absolute authority over matters pertaining to life on the rig.

Stratton engineers modified the crew quarters on the Voyager 7 for operations in Africa. They installed a second galley on the lower level and enlarged the cabins to permit a dormitory-style arrangement of 16 persons per room. This lower level of the rig makes up the "African section" of the rig, where the 120 local workers eat, sleep and socialize during their 28-day "hitch."

The upper level of the platform houses the 30 expatriates in an area equal in square footage to that of the African section. The "expatriate section" contains semi-private quarters with baths, and boasts its own galley, game room and movie room. Although not explicitly written, a tacit regulation exists prohibiting African workers from entering the expatriate section of the rig except in emergencies.

The only Africans exempt from this regulation are those assigned to the highly-valued positions of cleaning or galley staff in the expatriate section. The Africans hold these positions in high esteem because of the potential for receiving gifts or recovering discarded razors and other items from the expatriates.

Several other rig policies separate the African workers from the expatriates. African laborers travel to and from the rig by boat (an 18 hour trip), whereas expatriates receive helicopter transportation. An expatriate registered nurse dispenses medical attention to the expatriates throughout the day, but Africans have access to treatment only during shift changes or in an emergency. The two groups also receive disparate treatment when serious injuries arise. For instance, if a finger is severed, expatriates are rushed to the mainland for reconstructive surgery. However, due to the high cost of helicopter transportation, African workers must have an amputation operation performed on the rig by the medic.

The company issues gray coveralls to the Africans while the expatriates receive red coveralls. Meals in the two galleys are vastly different: the expatriate galley serves fine cuisine that approaches gourmet quality, while the Africans dine on a somewhat more proletarian fare. Despite the gross disparity in numbers served, the catering budgets for the two galleys are nearly equal.

Communication between the expatriates and the Africans is notably absent on the Voyager 7, since none of the expatriates speaks the native language and none of the Africans speaks more that a few words of the expatriates' language. Only the chef of the catering company knows both languages. Consequently, he acts as an interpreter in all emergency situations. In the every-day working environment, management must rely upon sign language or repetition of example to train and coordinate efforts.

From time to time an entourage of African government officials visits the Voyager 7. These visits normally last only for an hour or so. Invariably, the officials dine with the expatriates, take a brief tour of the equipment, and then return to shore by helicopter. No entourage has ever expressed concern about the disparity in living conditions on the rig, nor have officials ever bothered to speak with the African workers. Observers comment that the officials seem disinterested in the situation of the African workers, most of whom come from outside the capital city.

The presence of an expatriate black worker has little effect on the rig's segregated environment. The expatriate black is assigned to the expatriate section and partakes in all expatriate privileges. However, few expatriate blacks participate in the international drilling business and the few who do are frequently not completely welcomed into the rig's social activities.

You leave the oil rig feeling uneasy. You know that there has always been a disparity in living conditions on the drilling platforms. However, you want to make Stratton a socially responsible and profitable company. You wonder how you can best accomplish your dual goals.

THE CONFLICT AT LOMATEX CHEMICAL*

Case Summary

Your overseas marketing director has just landed a major contract with a North African nation for a large shipment of agricultural chemicals. You have reason to suspect that the foreign government may use your product to make weapons.

General Discussion Questions

1. Does a company have a moral responsibility to know how its product will be used in foreign countries?

2. Do companies have a moral obligation to contribute to the political stability of developing countries?

3. Should a company refuse to sell its products to countries that are led by ruthless dictators and/or are flagrant violators of the basic human rights of its people?

* Case written by Karen Marquiss.

THE CONFLICT AT LOMATEX CHEMICAL

You are the President of Lomatex Chemical, Inc., a medium-sized petrochemical company. The company manufactures a variety of chemical products for agricultural use, such as pesticides, herbicides, and fertilizers, along with a number of petroleum-based commodities.

Lomatex employs a large number of residents who live in the small community of about 40,000 where Lomatex is located. The firm enjoys a positive image in the area, and has been a stable economic force since the mid-1960s.

However, over the last few years, sales have consistently dropped in the industry. Luckily the company managed to weather the oil price instability of the 1980s. Still, the firm was forced to ride the ups and downs of the economy along with the rest of the industry. In order to temper these effects, you began to seek out new international markets for your agricultural products.

After a long search, you found the ideal person to head up the company's new international marketing division. Norman Smith was highly recommended by a number of your most respected colleagues. He had strong connections in Europe and Northern Africa from his days as marketing director with a competing firm. You decided to target the growing pesticide and fertilizer market in Africa. With a constant population growth, many of the developing African nations had a real need for agricultural products.

Only two months after he came on board, Norman had already landed a potentially lucrative contract. He solicited an attractive order from the government of Bawumba, a small nation located in north central Africa. The Bawumba officials wanted to purchase a small quantity of several agricultural chemicals in order to test them over a period of three months. If the results proved satisfactory, then the government would grant Lomatex a multimillion dollar contract for pesticides and fertilizers. It seemed like just the break that Lomatex needed to boost its sagging earnings. However, you decide to keep the good news a secret until the contract is signed.

On the very day you expect to hear from the Bawumban government, you receive a distressed call from Bill Swan, chief chemist from the pesticide division. You have always respected Bill and maintain an open-door policy with him and his staff.

As Bill enters your office, he seems distraught. Norman Smith had just leaked the news of the pending deal to him. Bill tells you that he spent some time in Bawumba in the foreign service, and that they could not possibly need a chemical shipment this large. When he was there 15 years ago, they had a good deal of agricultural production already under way; however, a large portion of the country is unsuitable for farming.

Bill reminds you that over the last two years, a new military dictatorship has taken power in Bawumba. Relations with their neighbors have become strained. He has even heard rumors of a possible arms buildup from friends who remain in the country. Bill warns you that chemical weaponry is common in that region, and that the government may use the Lomatex chemicals to produce poisonous gas.

You are stunned. The request from the Bawumbans seemed innocent enough. However, you do recall that over 200 Western firms had been accused of helping Iraq build up its supply of chemical and other weapons. Many of those Iraqi purchase orders appeared legitimate as well, and this fact did not release those companies from the responsibility of shipping potential weaponry to a hostile government. Recently, a number of Western firms were accused of jeopardizing their national interest.

On the one hand, you do not know if the Bawumbans have the technology to convert Lomatex chemicals into lethal weapons. Bill lived in the country many years ago. Perhaps technological development now permits the government to grow food on previously infertile land. On the other hand, you are not sure how the chemicals will be used.

As you ponder these concerns, the telephone rings. You answer, and Norman informs you that the Bawumba government has decided to grant Lomatex the contract.

THE MOZA ISLAND PROJECT*

Case Summary

Your firm is six months behind on a major construction project in the Middle East. You stand to lose up to $875,000 on the contract unless you make a "facilitating payment" to the government's contract administrator.

General Discussion Questions

1. Are there circumstances in which payments of this kind are questionable?

2. What does a manager do when his or her moral beliefs might cost the company a substantial loss of money?

3. How does one distinguish between a bribe, a gift and various kinds of facilitating payments?

*   Adapted by Karen Marquiss and Joanne B. Ciulla from "The Project at Moza Island," John A. Seeger and Balachandran Manyadarn, © Columbia University Graduate School of Business, 1991.

THE MOZA ISLAND PROJECT

The Project

You are owner and President of Gulf Trading Company. Your firm became involved in the Moza Island Project back in the early 1980s through collaboration with a large, influential multinational corporation located in the Middle East. The joint venture, known as Gulf Sargam, hoped to use Gulf Trading Company's contacts to secure large construction contracts. Meanwhile, the multinational provided all the technical, administrative and support staff, including the General Manager Joe Fernandes. Gulf Trading and the multinational had initially contributed capital of 51% and 49%, respectively, but profits were divided into 55% and 45% shares, respectively.

In January of 1983, the regional government decided to modernize the living facilities on Moza Island. Located 150 miles to the southeast of the nation's capital, Moza contained most of the country's major liquefied petroleum gas plants. The government invited bids from international construction firms in early 1983.

In April, the government awarded the mechanical subcontract to Gulf Sargam for $3 million. This contract amounted to almost ten times the company's original capital of $305,000. You felt that the estimated profit of $300,000 seemed dangerously low for a project spanning 18 months in a remote location. However, Joe, your General Manager, persuaded you to go ahead with the project because of the potential for future work. Joe then selected Tom Johnson to serve as Moza Island Project Manager for Gulf Sargam.

To protect its interests, the government employed a prominent consulting firm to supervise the Moza Island Project. Habib Sharif was Construction Consultant. He had final authority on every aspect of the project, including approvals of equipment, finish work, variations and change orders. Disagreements between the contractors and the construction consultant could only be resolved through a complex civil arbitration system administered by the government at its mainland capital.

Contract Execution

From the beginning, Tom, your Project Manager, noticed that Habib Sharif, the government's Construction Consultant, often went out of his way to enforce the contract specifications for Gulf Sargam. At Moza Island, Habib consistently interpreted contract clauses to the advantage of the government, insisting upon absolute compliance with even the smallest details. Habib routinely delayed Gulf Sargam's construction drawings and then returned them for correction of minute flaws. Only rarely did Habib approve Gulf's work the first time. In defense, Tom filed claims for reimbursement of the additional costs incurred by Gulf Sargam due to these delays.

On the other hand, Habib seemed extremely tolerant with the general contractor and each of the other subcontractors. He approved their work from his office without even visiting the job site. A year into the job, a space frame structure that was made of lightweight aluminum erected by the general contractor crashed to the ground. Fortunately, no one was hurt. Habib attributed the mishap to metal fatigue and not to shoddy workmanship.

A familiar picture began to unfold. Most construction consultants in the region expected to gain personally from their work, but none asked for an outright bribe. The consultant normally initiated the move with subtle "feelers" and awaited a response from the contractor. If a favorable reaction did not materialize, the consultant sent stronger signals, each causing more disruption to the contractor's work than the earlier one. However, Tom had faced this situation in several earlier projects and managed to avoid paying a bribe in each case through a combination of diplomacy and skill.

As owner and President of Gulf Trading Co., you had strong feelings on the subject. The fact that gratuities were often paid in the Middle East did not seem to you to make it right to pay them. The practice existed simply because corporations paid when asked. No law said that you must pay. Taking part in a corrupt system seemed immoral and served only to perpetuate the corruption. Giving in would set a precedent for all your other operations. You had to make it clear to Habib Sharif that the company would not play by those rules. Perhaps if you held fast, the man would see that you meant it. He would come around.

However, by June 1985, Gulf Sargam had incurred costs on an additional 9,000 man hours due to delays in approval of drawings and rejection of site work by Habib. Gulf had filed variation claims totalling $300,000, but not a single one had been approved. By early 1986, the delays imposed on the firm had slowed the entire Moza Island Project, but Habib refused to waver. Tom's crew found themselves six months behind schedule with the situation worsening every day.

At a chance meeting at the island club, Tom decided to confront Habib directly in order to resolve the matter before the end of the contract. Habib remarked that the general contractor and the other "subs" had taken "good care" of him and he had reciprocated their gesture accordingly. He expressed surprise that Gulf Sargam had not followed the same policy, a common Middle Eastern practice that remained essential for the smooth execution of a project.

But Habib claimed that it was not too late for Gulf Sargam. He had the authority to approve variation claims up to a total of $800,000 and Gulf Sargam could still make a profit. The cost of the consideration would equal $80,000, or ten percent of the claims approved for payment. Habib also pointed out that he had every right to enforce the contract agreement on Gulf Sargam, including an imposition of the contract's ten percent penalty clause should Gulf Sargam fail to complete the job on time. Tom repeated company policy on such financial arrangements, but said he would relay Habib's information to higher authorities.

Contract Completion

In June of 1986, you review this scenario. Gulf Sargam has completed the Moza Island contract six months behind schedule. Habib might impose the contract's penalty clause, adding another potential $300,000 to the firm's losses. Even without the penalty, your net loss amounts to $575,000 against an estimated profit of $300,000. Tom considered the situation hopeless. He said the firm must accede to Habib's request in order to recover its losses.

Joe Fernandes agreed. He reminded you that as an employee of the multinational he was obliged to take all possible steps to avoid losses to his parent company. Since Gulf Sargam had exhausted all other avenues, Joe told you to endorse the payment to Habib. He then underscored his government's interest in the performance of joint ventures. The government monitored financial results regularly, and a loss of this size would be difficult to explain. Joe's arguments are compelling but you do not feel comfortable with them.

DILLER'S DILEMMA:
STREET CHILDREN AND SUBSTANCE ABUSE*

Case Summary

C.E.O. Walter Diller faces a formidable problem. His firm's most profitable product is the drug of choice among Honduran street children. The firm's reputation for social responsibility is at risk.

General Discussion Questions

1. Is a company responsible for dangerous misuse of its product in a foreign location?

2. How much of an obligation does a company have to address serious social problems in developing countries?

3. Does a company have a moral obligation to challenge the laws that it thinks are not in the public interest in a foreign country?

* Adapted by Karen Marquiss and Joanne B. Ciulla from "H. B. Fuller in Honduras: Street Children and Substance Abuse," Norman Bowie and Stefanie Ann Lenway © Columbia University Graduate School of Business, 1991

148

DILLER'S DILEMMA:
STREET CHILDREN AND SUBSTANCE ABUSE

Walter Diller, Chief Executive Officer of J.G. Diller, Inc., faced a formidable problem. Could the company continue production of its most profitable adhesive product, Endurol, and at the same time manage to maintain its impeccable image for social responsibility?

The executives at J.G. Diller, Inc. first became aware of the substance abuse problem back in 1986 when Honduran newspapers carried articles about police arrests of street children who drugged themselves by sniffing glue. Most of the orphaned or runaway children lived in the poorest slums of the big cities where they scratched out a minimal existence as beggars and illegal squatters. The commonly available adhesive known as Endurol emerged as the substance of choice among these young junkies due to its low price and hallucinogenic qualities. The highly-addictive glue induced immediate feelings of elation, grandeur and power, but it also initiated irreversible liver and brain damage when used over a long period of time. Although the street children abused other substances in addition to Endurol, they soon became tagged as "Enduroleros," a name that eventually became synonymous with all street children, whether they used the drug or not.

Malena Chemical Industries, S.A., one of J.G. Diller's wholly-owned subsidiaries, first introduced Endurol to the Central American market in the early 1980s. Malena manufactured and distributed more than a dozen different adhesives under the Endurol brand name in several countries. In Honduras, where Endurol was manufactured, the products had a strong market position. The adhesives were intended primarily for use in shoe manufacturing and repair, leather work, and carpentry. The most common forms of Endurol had properties similar to those of airplane glue or rubber cement and were readily available at household goods stores throughout the country. Malena maintained tight control over the wholesale distribution of Endurol. Nearly all glue products that reached the Enduroleros came from retail outlets, either directly or through street pushers.

In spite of the competitive challenge of operating under unstable political and economic conditions in Central America, Malena managers stressed the objective of going beyond the bottom line in their annual report:

"Malena carries out business with the utmost respect for ethical and legal principles. Its orientation is not solely directed to the customer, who has the highest priority, but also to the shareholders, to employees, and to the communities where it operates."

Diller's founder and Chairman of the Board, J. Grant Diller, had become a legendary figure in the company's home area. He had served several terms in local government and remained active in civic affairs. Diller saw the company through four decades of financial success as President and Chief Executive Officer before handing over the managerial reins to his son Walter in January 1989.

Three months into Walter's term, angry letters began to trickle in from the stockholders. Some of these individuals heard of the Endurol problem through international press releases, while others had witnessed the problem first-hand in Central America. On November 2, 1989, Diller received an irate letter from a shareholder whose daughter worked with an international aid group in Honduras. The man demanded, "How can a company like J.G. Diller claim to have a social conscience and continue to sell Endurol which is practically burning out the brains of children in Latin America?" The letter's timing was uncanny. Walter was about to meet with a national group of socially responsible investors who were considering J.G. Diller's stock for inclusion in their portfolio.

Meanwhile, Walter learned that Malena management had failed to dissuade the Honduran government from regulating Endurol. As a solution to the glue sniffing problem, the legislature mandated that oil of mustard, allyl isothiocyanate, be added to Endurol to prevent its abuse. They argued that a person attempting to sniff glue with oil of mustard included would find it too powerful to tolerate, like getting an "overdose of horseradish." However, independent toxicology reports revealed that the oil of mustard had some acute side effects. The material could prove fatal if inhaled, swallowed or absorbed through the skin; it caused severe irritation or burns, and could destroy tissues of the mucous membranes, upper respiratory tract, eyes and skin. In addition, the Endurol with the oil of mustard included had a shelf life of only six months.

Given J.G. Diller's high visibility as a socially responsible corporation, the glue sniffing problem had the potential for becoming a public relations nightmare. Diller's staff suggested a number of options, including withdrawal of the product from the market or altering the formula to make Endurol a water-based product. Both would solve the glue-sniffing problem. However, any formula alteration would also affect the strength and durability of the glue, its most valuable properties.

Finally, Diller decided to go to Honduras and see what was going on. Upon his return, he realized that the situation involved more than product misuse and the company's image; it had social and community ramifications as well. The issue was substance abuse by children, regardless of who manufactured the product.

The depth of poverty in Honduras exacerbated the problem. In 1989, 65 percent of all households in Honduras lived in poverty, making it one of the poorest countries in Latin America. The government remained highly unstable with a large turnover rate. Officials usually settled for a quick fix. They seldom stayed in office long enough to manage a long term policy. By the time of Diller's trip, the oil-of-mustard law had been on the books for several months. However, officials had yet to implement the rule, and the country had scheduled national elections in three months.

Diller wondered if his company could do much to solve this complicated social problem.

NOTE ON THE CONTRIBUTORS

M. Cherif Bassiouni is Professor of Law and President of the International Human Rights Law Institute at DePaul University in Chicago.

Richard G. Capen, Jr. recently retired as Vice Chairman of Knight-Ridder, having joined the firm in 1979 as Senior Vice President and served as Chairman and Publisher of *The Miami Herald* for seven years. In 1992 he was appointed U.S. Ambassador to Spain.

Joanne B. Ciulla is the first holder of the Coston Family Chair in Leadership and Ethics in the Jepson School of Leadership Studies at the University of Richmond. From 1986 to 1990 she was a senior fellow in legal studies in management at The Wharton School at the University of Pennsylvania.

Richard T. De George is University Distinguished Professor of Philosophy and Courtesy Professor of Business Administration at the University of Kansas. He is past president of the American Philosophical Association (Central Division) and the Society for Business Ethics, and he currently heads the International Society of Business, Economics and Ethics.

Thomas Donaldson is the John Carroll Professor of Business Ethics in the School of Business, Georgetown University. He also holds the positions of Adjunct Professor in the Georgetown University Department of Philosophy, Senior Research Fellow at the Kennedy Institute of Ethics, and Senior Fellow of the Olsson Center for Ethics at the University of Virginia.

Wilfried Guth was Chief Executive of Deutsche Bank AG from 1976 to 1985. Currently he is a member of the Supervisory Board of Deutsche Bank and remains actively involved in a number of organizations concerned with international monetary policy and economic cooperation.

Shunji Hosaka has degrees in philosophy from Waseda University and Delhi University and currently is Research Scholar at The Eastern Institute, Inc. and a Lecturer at Tokai University.

Jack Mahoney is F. D. Maurice Professor of Moral and Social Theology at King's College in the University of London and Editor of *Business Ethics: A European Review*. In 1987 Professor Mahoney founded the King's College Business Ethics Research Centre, and since then his work as Director has included writing, broadcasting, consultancy and teaching at home and abroad in the field of business and management ethics.

Karen Marquiss is a doctoral student at The Wharton School of the University of Pennsylvania.

Paul M. Minus, principal founder of the Council for Ethics in Economics, has served as its President since 1988. Prior to joining the CEE staff, he taught at the Methodist Theological School in Ohio and at Florida State University.

Yukimasa Nagayasu is Professor at the International School of Economics and Business Administration, Reitaku University. Earlier he was Professor at the School of Social Science at Waseda University.

Stephen O'Brien is Executive Vice Chairman of Business in the Community, a national charity organization based in London. He also is Co-Founder and Chairman of Project Fullemploy, an organization established to assist in training of disadvantaged ethnic groups.

Amartya Sen is the Lamont University Professor at Harvard University and Professor of Economics and Philosophy. Before joining the Harvard faculty, Professor Sen taught at Oxford University, Cambridge University, Jadavpur University, Delhi University and the London School of Economics.

Meir Tamari is Director of the Institute of Ethics in Economics in Jerusalem, having earlier served as Chief Economist in the Office of the Governor of the Bank of Jerusalem.

Hiroyuki Yoshino joined Honda Motor Company, Ltd. in 1963, and between 1988 and 1991 he was President of Honda of America Mfg., Inc. He currently is Executive Vice President of Honda Motor Co., Ltd.

Issues in Business Ethics

1. G. Enderle, B. Almond and A. Argandoña (eds.): *People in Corporations*. Ethical Responsibilities and Corporate Effectiveness. 1991   ISBN: 0-7923-0829-8
2. B. Harvey, H. van Luijk and G. Corbetta (eds.): *Market, Morality and Company Size*. 1991   ISBN: 0-7923-1342-9
3. J. Mahoney and E. Vallance (eds.): *Business Ethics in a New Europe*. 1992   ISBN: 0-7923-1931-1
4. P. Minus (ed.): *The Ethics of Business in a Global Economy*. 1993   ISBN: 0-7923-9334-1